Great World Religions: Buddhism

Professor Malcolm David Eckel

THE TEACHING COMPANY ®

PUBLISHED BY:

THE TEACHING COMPANY
4151 Lafayette Center Drive, Suite 100
Chantilly, Virginia 20151-1232
1-800-TEACH-12
Fax—703-378-3819
www.teach12.com

ISBN 1-56585-805-0

Malcolm David Eckel, Ph.D.

Associate Professor of Religion, Boston University

Malcolm David Eckel received a B.A. in English from Harvard College in 1968. After a year at Episcopal Divinity in Cambridge, Massachusetts, he entered Oxford University to study Theology. He received his B.A. in Theology in 1971, with the M.A. to follow in 1975.

While he was in Oxford studying the classical sources of the Christian tradition, Professor Eckel took a long journey through the major pilgrimage sites of Turkey and Iran. Out of this experience grew a fascination with the religious traditions of the Middle East and the rest of Asia.

After studying Sanskrit at Oxford, Professor Eckel returned to Harvard for a Ph.D. in Comparative Religion with special emphasis on the Buddhist traditions of India, Tibet, and Southeast Asia. As part of this program, he spent a year of research at the Institute for Advanced Study of Sanskrit in Poona, a traditional center of Sanskrit learning near Bombay. During this year, he also came to know the scholars in the Tibetan refugee community in India. He completed his Ph.D. in 1980 with a dissertation on the Madhyamaka School of Indian Buddhist philosophy.

After teaching at Ohio Wesleyan University and at Middlebury College in Vermont, Professor Eckel returned to Harvard as an assistant professor. At Harvard, he taught courses on Buddhism and Comparative Religion and was involved in the programs of Harvard Divinity School. He served as lecturer on several Harvard alumni tours of South and Southeast Asia and as Acting Director of the Center for the Study of World Religions.

Professor Eckel tells his colleagues and friends that in 1990, at the end of his years at Harvard, he walked down to the Charles River, raised his staff, watched the waters part, and walked dryshod across the river to Boston University. The details of this story are clearly apocryphal, but the story expresses his satisfaction with the intellectual community he has found on the southern bank of the Charles River.

For the last decade at Boston University, Professor Eckel has taught courses on Buddhism, Comparative Religion, and the Religions of

Asia. He has also participated in the university's core curriculum program. In 1998, Professor Eckel received the Metcalf Award for Teaching Excellence, the university's highest award for teaching. In 2002, he was appointed the National Endowment for the Humanities Distinguished Teaching Professor of the Humanities.

In addition to many articles, Professor Eckel has published two books on Buddhist philosophy, including *To See the Buddha: A Philosopher's Quest for the Meaning of Emptiness*. He has traveled widely through the Buddhist countries of South, Southeast, and East Asia and is currently working on a book called *Metaphors Buddhist Live By*. This project explores the metaphorical connections between Buddhist thought and the practical demands of Buddhist life.

Table of Contents

Buddhism

Buddhism

Scope:

These 12 lectures survey the history of Buddhism—from its origin in India in the sixth and fifth centuries B.C.E. to the present day. They are meant to introduce students to the astonishing vitality and adaptability of a tradition that has transformed the civilizations of India, Southeast Asia, Tibet, China, Korea, and Japan and has now become a lively component in the cultures of the West.

Born as Siddhartha Gautama in a princely family in northern India about 566 B.C.E., the man who is known as the "Buddha," or the "Awakened One," left his family's palace and took up the life of an Indian ascetic. After years of difficult struggle, he sat down under a tree and "woke up" to the cause of suffering and to its final cessation. He then wandered the roads of India, preaching his *Dharma*, or "teaching"; gathering a group of disciples; and establishing a pattern of discipline that became the foundation of the Buddhist community, or *Samgha*. The Buddha helped his disciples analyze the causes of suffering and chart their own path to *nirvana*. Finally, after a long teaching career, he died and passed gently from the cycle of death and rebirth.

After the Buddha's death, the community's attention shifted from the Buddha himself to the teachings and moral principles embodied in his Dharma. Monks gathered to recite his teaching and produced a canon of Buddhist scripture, while disputes in the early community paved the way for the diversity and complexity of later Buddhist schools.

The Buddhist king Asoka, who reigned from about 268 to 239 B.C.E., sent the first Buddhist missionaries to Sri Lanka. From this missionary effort grew the *Theravada* ("tradition of the elders") Buddhism that now dominates all the Buddhist countries of Southeast Asia with the exception of Vietnam. Asoka also left behind the Buddhist concept of a "righteous king" who gives political expression to Buddhist values. This ideal has been embodied in recent times by King Mongkut in Thailand and Aung San Suu Kyi, who won the 1991 Nobel Peace Prize for her nonviolent resistance to military repression in Burma.

The Indian tradition was radically transformed by two major new movements. The first was known as the *Mahayana* ("Great

Vehicle"); the second, as *Tantra* or the *Vajrayana* ("Diamond Vehicle"). The Mahayana preached the ideal of the *bodhisattva* who postpones nirvana to help others escape the cycle of rebirth. Tantra developed a vivid and emotionally powerful method to achieve liberation in this life.

Buddhism entered Tibet in the seventh century and established itself as a powerful combination of Indian monasticism and *Tantric* practice. Tibetan Buddhism eventually developed four major schools, including the Geluk School of the Dalai Lama. Today, the fourteenth Dalai Lama carries Buddhist teaching around the world.

Buddhism entered China in the second century of the common era, at a time when the Chinese people had became disillusioned with traditional Confucian values. To bridge the gap between the cultures of India and China, Buddhist translators borrowed Taoist vocabulary to express Buddhist ideas. Buddhism took on a distinctively Chinese character, becoming more respectful of duties to the family and the ancestors, more pragmatic and this-worldly, and more consistent with traditional Chinese respect for harmony with nature. During the T'ang Dynasty (618–907), Buddhism was expressed in a series of brilliant Chinese schools, including the Ch'an School of meditation that came to be known in Japan as Zen.

Buddhism entered Japan in the sixth century of the Common Era and soon became allied with the power of the Japanese state. Buddhist Tantra was given distinctive Japanese expression in the Shingon School, and the Tendai School brought the sophisticated study of Chinese Buddhism to the imperial court. During the Kamakura period (1192–1333), Japan suffered wide social and political unrest. Convinced that they were living in a "degenerate age," the brilliant reformers Honen (1133–1212), Shinran (1173–1262), and Nichiren (1222–1282) brought a powerful new vision of Buddhism to the masses. The Kamakura period also saw a series of charismatic Zen masters who gave new life to the ancient tradition of Buddhist meditation.

Lecture One
Buddhism as a World Religion

Scope:

During its 2,500-year history, from the time of the Buddha to the present day, Buddhism has grown from a tiny religious community in northern India into a movement that now spans the globe. It has shaped the development of civilization in India and Southeast Asia; significantly influenced the civilizations of China, Tibet, Korea, and Japan; and has become a major part of the multi-religious world in Europe and North America. Although Buddhism plays the role of a "religion" in many cultures, it challenges some of our most basic assumptions about religion. Buddhists do not worship a God who created and sustains the world. They revere the memory of a human being, Siddhartha Gautama, who found a way to be free from suffering and bring the cycle of rebirth to an end. For Buddhists, this release from suffering constitutes the ultimate goal of human life.

Outline

I. When you come to Buddhism after studying other major religious traditions, you have to be prepared for some surprises.

    A. Many aspects of Buddhism seem very familiar.

        1. For example, Buddhists tell a story about the founder of their tradition. His name was Siddhartha Gautama. He lived in northern India around 500 B.C.E. and was known to his followers as the Buddha, or the "Awakened One." Like Jesus and Muhammad, he developed a distinctive response to the religious problems of his day, and he started a religious movement that now spans the globe, from India and Southeast Asia; to China, Tibet, Korea, and Japan; and in the last hundred years, to Europe, North America, and other parts of the world.

        2. During his life, the Buddha created an order of monks and nuns who passed on a tradition of Buddhist learning and practice, as Christian monks and nuns did in Europe during the Middle Ages and still do in many parts of the Christian world today.

3. Buddhists have familiar patterns of ritual and worship. They go on pilgrimages to important shrines; they worship images and sites that are sacred to the Buddha; and they mark the stages of life with rites of passage, similar to the ritual of a *bar mitzvah* in Judaism or baptism in Christianity.

4. Buddhists also teach people how to confront and deal with the deepest questions of human life: What will happen to me when I die? How can I live my life in a way that will be happy, peaceful, compassionate, and free from suffering?

B. But some aspects of Buddhism challenge our assumptions about religion.

1. *Webster's New Collegiate Dictionary* defines religion as "the service and adoration of God or a god expressed in forms of worship." If you mention the word "religion" to most people, the first idea that comes to mind is "God." There are gods in Buddhism, and Buddhists sometimes attribute special powers to the Buddha, but the tradition begins simply with a human being—Siddhartha Gautama—who found a solution to the problem of human suffering. Buddhists focus on his experience, and they deny the existence of a single, almighty God.

2. The Buddhist tradition will challenge us to look in new ways at some basic religious questions: What is ultimate reality? How can I know it? And does it love me?

3. Many religious traditions emphasize the importance of an immortal soul. This is not so in Buddhism. Buddhists say that a human personality is like a river or a raging fire: The personality is constantly changing, and the idea of an immortal soul is simply an illusion that human beings impose on a process of constant change. Buddhist ideas of the self challenge us to think in new ways about some old questions: Who am I? How can I develop my full potential as a human being?

4. What is true for human beings is also true for Buddhism itself. Like everything else in the world, Buddhism is constantly changing. As we consider the astonishing variety of Buddhism that evolved in India and elsewhere in Asia, we will have to ask ourselves: What actually is

Buddhism? Are there any values, practices, or religious commitments that remain constant through this extraordinary process of cultural change?

II. The most basic Buddhist expression of faith is called the "triple refuge": "I take refuge in the Buddha; I take refuge in the *Dharma* [the Buddha's teaching]; I take refuge in the *Samgha* [the community of the Buddha's followers]." We will take our first step into the world of Buddhism by looking at each of these three refuges.

   A. We begin, of course, with the Buddha himself, the "Awakened One" who set the Buddhist tradition in motion.
      1. The Buddha often is depicted sitting in a serene pose, with feet crossed in front of him and hands folded in his lap—the very picture of calm and contemplation. This is the image that has drawn people to the Buddha for many centuries, and it is the one that conveys most explicitly the experience of his awakening.
      2. After his awakening, the Buddha got up from his seat and taught his experience to others on the roads of northern India. The major events of the Buddha's life took place in the Madhyadesha, or the "Middle Region," of the Ganges Basin in northern India. These sites are still the focus of Buddhist pilgrimage today.

   B. The Buddha's Dharma, or "teaching," is often expressed by Four Noble Truths: the truths of suffering, the origin of suffering, the cessation of suffering (or *nirvana*), and the truth of the path to the cessation of suffering. These will be the subjects of our third and fourth lectures.

   C. The fifth lecture will take up some of the important institutional issues that confronted the Buddhist community after the death of the Buddha, including the origins of monasticism and the development of a canon of Buddhist scripture.

III. After laying the foundations for our study of Buddhism, we will trace the development of Buddhism through India, Southeast Asia, Tibet, China, and Japan.

   A. In India itself, two major reform movements appeared that changed the face of Buddhism. The first of these was called the *Mahayana*, or "Great Vehicle." The second was called *Tantra*. The word *Tantra* is difficult to translate, but we might think of it, for the moment at least, as "power." We will explore the Mahayana and Tantric traditions in separate lectures.

B. As Buddhism was transmitted to other countries in Asia, it developed in strikingly new ways.

1. Buddhism was carried to Sri Lanka (the island that used to be called Ceylon) by Buddhist missionaries in the third century B.C.E. From Sri Lanka, it was carried to much of Southeast Asia, including Indonesia.

2. Buddhism entered China in the second century C.E., carried north by monks and merchants over the mountains of Central Asia and across the Silk Road into the heartland of China.

3. From China, Buddhism was eventually carried to Korea, Japan, and Vietnam.

4. In the eighth century, Buddhism was carried across the Himalayas from India to Tibet. Today, the Dalai Lama, the leader of the Tibetan Buddhist community, is one of the most visible and active Buddhist leaders in the world. In many ways, he is living symbol not just of Tibetan Buddhism, but of Buddhism itself.

5. We will give separate attention to the major varieties of Buddhism in all these cultural areas in our final four lectures.

C. Today, Buddhism has spread through much of the rest of the world, including Europe, Australia, and the Americas.

1. In some places, Buddhism is strongest in ethnic communities, such as the Sri Lankan Buddhist Samgha in Los Angeles or the Buddhist Churches of America, a Japanese-based community on the West Coast and in Hawaii.

2. Buddhism also has had wide influence through several generations of Western converts.

D. These lectures have two goals:

   1. To give you a sophisticated appreciation of the varieties of Buddhism in the world, not just as historical movements but in the present day.

   2. To look at the world through Buddhist eyes and imagine what it might be like to be part of the unfolding historical drama we know by the name of "Buddhism."

   3. In the process of achieving these two goals, we will find that Buddhism challenges the way we look at religion. It will challenge us to ask some familiar questions in a new way: What is sacred to us, what is our ultimate concern, and how are religious values reflected in our society? If we approach this tradition with an open mind and an open heart, the "otherness" of Buddhism will give us a new way of understanding ourselves.

Essential Reading:

Robinson and Johnson, *The Buddhist Religion*, Introduction.

Supplementary Reading:

Brown, *Man in the Universe*.

Questions to Consider:

1. When you attempt to understand a new religious tradition, what is the most important thing to learn? Would you focus on its doctrines, the way it tells stories, its art, its rituals, or its institutions? Would you focus on something else?

2. If you were trying to explain your own religious tradition to someone who knew nothing about it, what would be the most important thing for that person to learn?

Lecture One—Transcript
Buddhism as a World Religion

Welcome to our twelve-lecture introductory course on the study of Buddhism. We've put this course together so that we can understand and study the Buddhist tradition in the context of a larger comparative course on the Great Religious Traditions of the World, so that we can see some of the distinctive things about the Buddhist experience in the larger context of the religious experience of human beings more generally.

I should say to you right at the very beginning that the Buddhist tradition is particularly close to my heart. I've spent most of my adult life exploring the twists and turns in Buddhist traditions across the continent of Asia, and also in Buddhist communities here in North America. I find Buddhism endlessly fascinating, and I'm delighted to be able to share some of that fascination with you.

When you come to Buddhism after you've been studying many of the other major religious traditions in the world, you have to be prepared for some significant surprises. Many aspects of Buddhism will seem familiar to you. Buddhists tell a story, like Christians or Muslims, about the founder of their tradition. His name was Siddhartha Gautama. He lived in northern India around 500 years or so before the Common Era. He was known to his followers as the Buddha, or the "Awakened One."

Like Jesus and Muhammad, he developed a very distinctive response to the religious problems of his day. He started a religious movement that now spans the globe, from India and Southeast Asia, across northern Asia to China, Japan, Korea, and Tibet, and in the last hundred years or so to Europe, North America, and other parts of the world.

You might ask yourselves at the beginning of our discussion together, how the Buddha, as a founder of a religious tradition, differs from other founders. Jesus and Muhammad brought messages, as if they were people communicating some sort of a message from divine reality that their followers were then meant to heed and respond to. The Buddha, unlike Jesus and Muhammad, serves more as an example. It isn't that he brings a divine message. He gives us an example of behavior that we as human beings are invited to follow in order to achieve a goal that's very similar to the goal that he achieved in his own life.

The Buddha also put together a community of followers like other major founders of other significant religious traditions. In his case, it was an order of monks and nuns who passed on a tradition of Buddhist learning and practice just as the Christian monks and nuns did in Europe in the Middle Ages and in many parts of the Christian world today. During our course we'll get some sense of how this society of monks and nuns operates and how it establishes its relationships with Buddhist kings and queens and princes and all of the ordinary laypeople who make up the structure of Buddhist society.

Buddhists also have very familiar patterns of ritual and worship. They go on pilgrimages to important shrines. Just a few years ago I was in Tibet and joined a group of really remarkable pilgrims from eastern Tibet who went up to one of the major mountain peaks in central Tibet and circumambulated around the mountain peak to pay homage to the different shrines that were associated with different saints at each point along the route. These pilgrimages are not unlike the sacred pilgrimages that occur in the Christian tradition, a pilgrimage to Lourdes for example, or a pilgrimage to some of the great holy sites in eastern Europe.

Buddhists also mark the stages of life with rites of passage, like baptism in Christianity or a *bar mitzvah* in Judaism. We'll be looking in the course of our study at these patterns of ritual, worship, pilgrimage, rites of passage that make Buddhists' life distinctive, and pass on the teaching of the Buddha. In our own way, we'll make a pilgrimage of our own as we move across Asia studying the different aspects of the Buddhist tradition in different countries of Asia.

Buddhists also teach people how to confront and deal with some of the deepest questions of Buddhist life, not unlike people in other religious traditions. They're concerned about issues that confront all of us as human beings: What will happen to me when I die? How can I live in a way that will be happy, peaceful, compassionate, and free from suffering? These are questions that concern all of us as human beings. Buddhists have distinctive, and in many respects very powerful, answers to these questions.

All of these are familiar issues, issues that we have encountered in one way or another in other religious traditions. I suspect we've encountered them whether we've studied those religious traditions in a formal sense or not. Some aspects of Buddhism will challenge our assumptions about the nature of religion itself.

When I start out the study of Buddhism with my students at Boston University, I hand out, on a piece of paper, a standard dictionary definition of religion that I've taken from a dictionary that I've used for years since I was a college student. It goes, "Religion is the service and adoration of God, or a god, expressed in forms of worship." I suspect that, if I could ask you to jot down in an intuitive sense, in a very quick way what you think religion is, the word "God" would appear somewhere in that definition.

Buddhists do worship gods. Gods are a part of Buddhist life, gods are important in some aspects of Buddhist ritual, but Buddhists deny the existence of one single almighty powerful God who created the world. The Buddha is simply a human being just like us, who confronted some of the great difficulties of life and worked out a human response.

When we study Buddhism as part of the religious traditions of the world, as one of the major religious traditions in a series like this, we have to confront the possibility that religion can be worked out on the deepest level without a concern for a creator, God. That will challenge our understanding of what religion itself is.

Buddhists instead ask questions like this: What is ultimate reality? What does it mean for something to be ultimately real? How can I know it? Does it, in the end, love me?—that great religious question in a Buddhist form.

Another aspect of Buddhism that will be surprising and challenging to us has to do with the nature of the self. Many religious traditions emphasize the importance of an immortal soul. If you've encountered as part of this larger course, or in some other context, the Hindu tradition, you know that for Hindus identifying the nature of the immortal soul and finding some way to separate that soul from the confusion of ordinary, everyday experiences, is one of the crucial goals of human life.

This is not so in Buddhism, Buddhists say that a human personality is a bit like a river, constantly flowing, or like a fire that's constantly burning. The soul itself is not eternal. It doesn't endure. It's constantly part of a changeable process. The idea of an immortal soul is simply an illusion that we as human beings impose out of our own psychological or emotional needs on a process of constant change.

Buddhist ideas of the self will challenge us to think in new ways about some basic questions, some questions that belong to all of us as human beings: Who am I? What am I really? How can I develop my full potential as a human being? What's true for human beings, of course, is also true for Buddhism itself. Like everything else in the world, Buddhism is constantly changing, and, as we consider in our own study together in this twelve-lecture series the astonishing varieties of Buddhism that evolved in India and elsewhere in Asia, we'll have to ask ourselves another set of questions: What actually is Buddhism? What do we mean by that word? Are there any values, practices, or religious commitments that remain constant through this extraordinary process of cultural change? These are questions that come up in a particularly sharp form in the study of Buddhism, but they really apply to all of the other religious traditions in the world, as well.

These are the challenges that lie ahead of us in this twelve-lecture series. If these are our questions, how should we organize our study of Buddhism so that we can tackle them in the most direct and effective way? I think we have to take some guidance from Buddhists themselves. The most basic Buddhist expression of faith, one that's very commonly repeated when Buddhists perform their daily devotions or when a person begins to express a Buddhist identity and loyalty to the Buddhist tradition, is called the triple refuge: I take refuge in the Buddha, I take refuge in the *Dharma*, which is the Buddha's teaching, and I take refuge in the *Samgha*, which is the community of the Buddha's disciples.

We will take our first step into the world of Buddhism by looking at each one of these three refuges. We'll begin, of course, with the Buddha himself, the Awakened One, who set the Buddhist tradition in motion. The Buddha, as many of you know, is often depicted sitting in a very serene posture, with his feet crossed in front of him and his hands folded in his lap. The pose is called in the terminology of traditional yoga, the lotus position. It's the very picture of calm contemplation, this is the classic image of the Buddha and it's the image that has drawn many people to the Buddha for many centuries across the continent of Asia and here today in North America. It's the one that conveys most explicitly the experience of his awakening, and it also is an image that Buddhists try to recreate in their own experience. A really useful starting point for us now, as we begin our study of Buddhism, might be to try to recreate that experience a bit for ourselves.

I'm told by the people who have organized these marvelous lectures that many people listen to the courses of The Teaching Company on tape when they're commuting through rush hour traffic in the morning. If that's true for you, as you listen to this course, take the image of the Buddha. Place him in some way in front of you. Don't be distracted too much because you need to keep your eyes on the road, but just place that image of the Buddha in front of you and try to absorb some of the calm and contemplation that comes from that figure. This is a perfect starting point for our study of the tradition, and it's not a bad image to have in mind actually as you're creeping your way down some smog-choked interstate or freeway on the way to work in the morning. This is one of the aspects of the Buddhist tradition that is extremely attractive, and it's one from which we have so much to learn.

The Buddha is an image of calm, of serenity, in a confused and distracting world. The Buddha, of course, didn't remain in the lotus position for his entire adult life. He did have to get up at a certain point and walk across northern India and encounter people who eventually in time became his disciples and began to band together and create the religious community that has carried his teaching on to the present day.

The major events of the Buddha's life took place in a region that's called the Madhyadesha, or the "Middle Region" of the Ganges Basin in northern India. These sites are still the focus of Buddhists' pilgrimage today. We'll walk through some of those sites, at least imaginatively, in our own study of this tradition, walking in our own way in the footsteps of the Buddha.

The second of the three refuges has to do with the Buddha's Dharma, or teaching. This teaching is often expressed in a doctrinal formula known as The Four Noble Truths: the truth of suffering; the origin of suffering; the cessation of suffering or *nirvana*, a commonly known Buddhist word; and the fourth truth, the truth of the path to the cessation of suffering. These will be the subjects of our third and fourth lectures after we've discussed the life of the Buddha. The fifth lecture will take up some of the important institutional issues that confronted the Buddhist community after the death of the Buddha, including the origins of monasticism and the development of a cannon of Buddhist scripture. All of these are issues that have deeply shaped the form of Buddhist institutions—from the time of the Buddha right straight through to the present day.

After we've laid the foundations for our study of Buddhism we'll trace the development of the tradition through India, Southeast Asia, Tibet, China, and Japan. I'll just mention a few of the major movements that we'll want to encounter as we trace the tradition along this geographical trajectory. In India itself, there were two major reform movements that appeared in early Buddhist history that changed the face of the tradition. The first of these was called the *Mahayana*, or "Great Vehicle" that emerged rather mysteriously right around the beginning of the Common Era, and eventually involved a massive reorganization of basic Buddhist values.

The second movement was called *Tantra*, and we'll spend a little bit of time as we move on to this tradition talking about what that word means. It's actually quite ambiguous. I think it probably makes most sense for us now simply to say that the word *Tantra* means "power" because the Tantra tradition is one that has to do with accumulating power and using it in some way to serve the interests of people in this world. We'll explore the Mahayana and the Tantric traditions in separate lectures.

As Buddhism was transmitted to other countries in Asia, it also continued to develop in quite striking ways. Buddhism was carried to Sri Lanka, the island that used to be called Ceylon, by Buddhist missionaries in the third century before the Common Era. From Sri Lanka, it was carried to much of Southeast Asia, including Indonesia. There's not much Buddhism present in Indonesia anymore, although there are some important echoes of the Buddhist tradition on the island of Bali. As you travel around Indonesia today some of the most extraordinary Buddhist monuments in the world are still preserved. On the island of Java there's a monument known as Borobudur, a great Buddhist shrine that was constructed late in the Mahayana period in the development of the tradition that I think is probably one of the greatest Buddhist monuments in the world, still preserved there on the central island in Indonesia.

We'll be talking a bit about the development of the tradition in Southeast Asia, its spread from Sri Lanka and its expansion through Burma and through Thailand, and consider at least briefly some of the modern examples of Buddhism in those cultures today.

Buddhism entered China in the second century of the Common Era, carried north across the Silk Road, through the Khyber Pass or over some of the other great passes of the Himalayas, on through Afghanistan and then across the Silk Road into northern China, and developed some remarkably distinctive traditions in an interaction with the indigenous traditions of China. China is—and has been for many, many centuries—a supremely confident and bold cultural tradition and didn't take very easily at all to the introduction of Buddhism. It was considered a foreign tradition and for that reason rather suspect.

However, there was a certain kind of extraordinary affinity between Buddhist teaching and an aspect of Chinese culture that goes by the name of *Taoism*. The Taoist tradition has been for centuries one of the vibrant aspects of Chinese culture, and, because of that natural affinity with this aspect of Chinese culture, Buddhism was able to move in a way that almost in retrospect seems effortless into Chinese culture; began to interact with Chinese cultural forms and develop a very distinctive form of Buddhism that is Chinese in character. That form of Buddhism was eventually carried to Korea and to Japan, Zen Buddhism is an example of what I'm talking about, and then on into Vietnam where the Buddhist traditions are largely Chinese in origin. In the eighth century, Buddhism was carried across the Himalayas from India to Tibet.

Today, the Dalai Lama, who is the leader of the Tibetan Buddhist community, is one of the most visible and active Buddhist leaders in the world. In many ways he's not just a living symbol of Tibetan Buddhism, but a symbol of Buddhism itself. We'll have a chance, in one of our lectures at least, to look at some of the very distinctive characteristics of Tibetan Buddhism. It's extraordinarily colorful and challenging in many of the ways that it functions in spite of the fact that Tibet is, in many ways, one of the smallest of the Buddhist countries of Asia, certainly in population.

Tibetan Buddhism has extraordinary prestige and power because of its intellectual sophistication and its ritual drama. We'll have a chance to talk a bit about that and about what it is that makes Tibetan

Buddhism so remarkably colorful and attractive as a variety of Buddhism in the world today. We'll be giving separate attention to all the major varieties of Buddhism in all these different cultural areas in our last four lectures, ending with a lecture on the Buddhism of Japan.

Buddhism has spread through much of the rest of the world, including Europe, Australia, and the Americas. In some places in this country, Buddhism is strongest in ethnic communities, such as the Sri Lankan Buddhist Samgha in Los Angeles, or the Buddhist Churches of America, which is a Japanese-based Buddhist organization on the West Coast and in Hawaii. Buddhism also has had tremendous influence through several generations of Western converts to the tradition, as Zen masters and Tibetan Buddhist teachers and meditation masters from Southeast Asia have brought their traditions to the West.

If we cast the net even wider, it's clear that Buddhist values have had tremendous impact on all sorts of areas of American society: on film, on poetry, on the visual arts, and even on sports as the martial arts have become appropriated by athletes as a way to train the mind and body for athletic competition. It's clear that one of our most important goals in these lectures will be simply to survey the different types of Buddhism available in the world so that you can become wise observers yourselves and wise interpreters of this tradition that has now become such a lively part of our multicultural world.

The course is not meant, in the end, just to be a survey. One of my most respected colleagues in the study of religion says that we study religious traditions like Buddhism to encounter the other and interrogate the familiar. For many of you, Buddhism will be a completely new experience. Even if you've grown up as a Buddhist and are familiar with Buddhist values, a lot of what we discuss will very likely be new even to you, and it will give you new ways of looking at your own tradition. Either way, it's important to be aware of how different Buddhism is in the way it approaches the basic issues of human life. Encountering the otherness of Buddhism is a crucial part of the process of understanding.

Buddhists really do look at the world in a different way, and we have to be sensitive to the differences if we want to understand them. However, the process of understanding is not complete unless we bring it back home and look at ourselves through Buddhist eyes. Buddhism will challenge the way we look at religion. It will ask us to think in new ways about what's sacred to us. What stories do we tell about the nature of human life? What's their origin? How do we find some way to enact them in our own experience so that it gives our own experience a new sense of texture and meaning? What sacred places do we go to that remind us in some way of experiences that have been important in the origins of our tradition? What rituals do we use? How do we mark the stages of life and the passage from one important aspect of human experience to another?

Buddhism has to do, in many respects, with being sensitive to the sacred dimension of human experience, and it will ask us to look back on our own experience and our own religious traditions to see in new ways how people articulate a sense of the sacred and attempt to incorporate it into their own experience. It also will ask us to think in new ways about how we encounter what is of ultimate concern to us. The great theologian Paul Tillich once said that religion has to do with the state of being grasped by an ultimate concern. For many religious people, they encounter the religious dimension of life when they come face-to-face with something that challenges them to think about the ultimate significance of their experience and about their lives. The Buddhist tradition will do this in ways that may very well be new to us, especially because they don't mediate this question through the concept of God as it is mediated in so many of the religious traditions that we know of that are closer to home.

Buddhists will also force us to see in a new way the social dimension of religion. Buddhist values come to us initially as being very personal, very much having to do with the interior life, with attitudes of mind and states of the soul, in which people attempt to reorient themselves toward issues that are of particular concern to them and free themselves from the distraction and the suffering that afflicts ordinary human life. Yet Buddhist values, like the values of other religious traditions, have often been drawn into complex social and political dynamics, so at a certain point in our course, when we study the developments of Buddhism in Southeast Asia, we'll look very closely at the way the relationship between Buddhist monks and Buddhist kings gave a certain political and social spin to the Buddhist tradition that makes it rather distinctive as one of the religious traditions of Asia. This will challenge us again to look at the political and social significance of many of the religious traditions that we're aware of closer to home.

I hope that Buddhism will press us a little bit to become more aware of the religious dimension of experience as it is familiar in the world around us. It would be a bit presumptuous of me to think at the beginning of this course that I will somehow make you a Buddhist during the course of our lectures. I wouldn't hold out that hope. It seems to me unrealistic and inappropriate in an academic setting like this. However, I do hope that these lectures will help you become more wise and more active interpreters of the religious values that are close to home. I hope in this way that the course will deepen and enrich your appreciation of religious experience wherever you encounter it. I'm certainly looking forward to these lectures and I hope very much that you are too.

Lecture Two
The Life of the Buddha

Scope:

The history of Buddhism began in India in the sixth century B.C.E. with the birth of Siddhartha Gautama, the man who is known as the "Awakened One," or Buddha. After being raised in luxury, Siddhartha Gautama saw four sights that impressed him with the problem of suffering, death, and reincarnation. He left his family's palace and set out to find a solution. After difficult study and practice, he "woke up" to the truth and became the Buddha. He then walked the roads of northern India, attracting a group of disciples and establishing a model of practice for the Buddhist community. Around the age of 80, he achieved his "perfect nirvana," passing beyond the cycle of death and rebirth. His life has given rise to a rich tradition of stories that tell us not only about Buddhist origins but also about Buddhist aspirations for a life of wisdom, freedom, and peace.

Outline

I. When a person encounters Buddhism for the first time, it is natural to ask two questions:

    A. Who was the Buddha? How did the story of the Buddha become woven into the lives of the people who call themselves Buddhists?

    B. This lecture will do two things:

        1. Tell the life story of the Buddha.

        2. Reflect about the way that story has been mirrored in the lives of Buddhist people throughout Asia and the rest of the world.

II. Historians are confident of a few key facts about the Buddha's life:

    A. He was born into the family of King Shuddhodana and Queen Maya about the year 566 B.C.E. in a region of the Indian subcontinent that now lies in southern Nepal. (This date has been questioned recently by a group of historians who place his birth in the fifth century B.C.E.)

        1. He was a member of the Shakya tribe; his clan name was Gautama; and his given name was Siddhartha.

2. It is common to refer to him as Siddhartha Gautama or, more commonly, as Shakyamuni, "The Sage of the Shakya Tribe."

B. These facts tell us that the Buddha was not a figment of someone's imagination: He was a real human being. But they do not tell us much about what the Buddha did or about the impact he had on his followers. To learn about the Buddha this way, we must turn to the stories Buddhists tell about the Buddha.

III. Buddhists have a rich tradition of stories and legends about the Buddha.

A. The stories begin with the Buddha's previous lives.

B. Buddhist tradition arose at a time when the doctrine of reincarnation was a basic assumption in Indian religious life.
   1. The doctrine of reincarnation or rebirth is known as *samsara* (literally, "wandering").
   2. Samsara was not considered a pleasant prospect. For many people, it was not an opportunity as much as it was a burden, and they tried to find a way out.

C. Stories about the Buddha's previous lives are told in texts known as *Jataka*, or "Birth Tales."
   1. Most of these stories convey simple moral lessons, often in a form that is accessible to children.
   2. An example is the story of the monkey, the elephant, and the partridge.
   3. In a technical sense, these stories are not yet about the Buddha but about a "future Buddha," known as a *bodhisattva*.

D. Stories about the Buddha's life contain several key episodes. These episodes are widely represented in Buddhist art and have had an important influence on the way Buddhists imagine an ideal human life.
   1. The birth of the future Buddha was surrounded by miraculous signs indicating that he would become a *chakravartin*, or a "turner of the wheel." A chakravartin becomes either a great king and turns the wheel of conquest or a religious teacher and turns the wheel of *Dharma*, or religious teaching. The wheel of the Dharma has become the international symbol of Buddhism.

2. Siddhartha's father tried to protect him from the suffering of the world in the hope that he would become a great king. He was raised as a prince, was married, and had a child.

3. In his early thirties, he traveled outside the palace and saw four sights: a sick person, an old person, a corpse, and an ascetic. These sights inspired him to renounce life in the palace and become an ascetic. His renunciation or ("going forth") is reenacted in Buddhist communities today whenever a young person becomes a monk or nun.

4. He began the path of renunciation with severe fasting and self-discipline. Eventually, he found that this was unproductive, and he adopted a mode of discipline known as the Middle Path, avoiding the extremes of self-denial and self-indulgence. The theme of the Middle Path has affected not only Buddhist discipline but also the way Buddhists think about fundamental questions, such as the nature of the self.

5. Following this mode of discipline, the future Buddha sat down under a tree and, with intense meditation, woke up to the truth. With this experience, he became a Buddha, someone who has "awakened" from the dream of ignorance and whose wisdom has "blossomed" like a flower.

6. When Siddhartha became a Buddha, he also achieved the state or the goal that Buddhists call *nirvana*, which means "to extinguish" or "to blow out." A Buddha is someone who has understood the causes of suffering and has "blown them out," meaning that he no longer suffers from the ignorance and desire that feed the fire of death and rebirth.

7. The Buddha got up from the tree of his awakening, walked to Sarnath, in the outskirts of Banaras, and turned the wheel of his Dharma by preaching about his realization to a small group of his former companions.

8. Among the many stories about this phase of the Buddha's life is a strange story about Angulimala ("Garland of Fingers"), a serial killer who collected his victims' fingers. He met the Buddha, was stricken with

remorse, and became a member of the Buddha's monastic community.

9. Another story of the Buddha's teaching, which became popular in China, has to do with his transmission of the Dharma to Kashyapa, not by words, but by holding up a flower.

10. These stories show something about the Buddha and something about the Buddhist tradition. Words have their place, but the Buddha's teaching also can be conveyed through gestures, a smile, a tilt of the head, or perhaps best of all, through silence. Buddhism is a teaching about the way to live a serene and contemplative life. The Buddha taught this as much by his example as by his words.

11. At the age of about 80, after a long and productive teaching career, the Buddha lay down between two trees and passed gently from the realm of death and rebirth. This event is called his *parinirvana* or Complete Extinction.

12. After the Buddha's death, his body was cremated, and his relics were enshrined in reliquary mounds, or *stupas*. These stupas became the models for the practice of Buddhist worship.

E. Buddhists follow the example of the Buddha by walking, literally or metaphorically, in his footsteps, by attempting to wake up to the truth and extinguish the fires of desire and dissatisfaction.

Essential Reading:
Robinson and Johnson, *The Buddhist Religion*, ch. 1.

Supplementary Reading:
Strong, *The Experience of Buddhism*, ch. 1.

Questions to Consider:

1. The story of the Buddha is so familiar that it is easy to take it for granted, but it represents a distinctive cultural image of an ideal human life. Are there any features of the story that seem surprising or problematic?

2. The concept of freedom is a central value in many cultures. Do you think that the story of the Buddha gives a convincing picture of freedom?

Lecture Two—Transcript
The Life of the Buddha

When someone encounters Buddhism for the first time, when you come as we do as students to this tradition, beginning to ask some basic questions about the study of Buddhism, the most natural question to ask is simply: Who was the Buddha? Who was that man? Who is the person who set this incredibly rich and complex religious tradition in motion?

If you're at all curious about the impact that this person had on the lives of the people in India where he was born and in all the other countries in Asia—including modern America, where Buddhism has become an important part of the religious landscape—it's also natural to ask another question: How did the life story of this person, the person we call the Buddha, become so deeply woven into the lives of the people who call themselves Buddhists?

In our second lecture I'd like to do two things, I'd like to tell you the story of the Buddha's life, and also reflect about the way that story has been mirrored in the lives of Buddhist people throughout Asia and today in our own communities in North America.

Historically, we have just a couple of facts about the life of the Buddha. We know, or we think we know, that he was born in the family of King Shuddhodana and Queen Maya about the year 566 B.C.E., in a region of the Indian subcontinent that now lies in what we would call southern Nepal. This date of 566 B.C.E. has been questioned recently by historians who place his birth a little bit later in the fifth century. I suppose we have to recognize right at the very beginning that there's a little bit of uncertainty about the Buddha's date, perhaps give or take about 50 years.

This young man was a member of the Shakya tribe. His clan name was Gautama. His given name was Siddhartha, which means something like "goal achieved," or "mission accomplished." It's been common in the Buddhist world to refer to him as Siddhartha Gautama, or even more commonly as Shakyamuni, "The Sage of the Shakya Clan."

This handful of historical facts is actually important to us. They tell us that the Buddha was not a figment of someone's imagination. He was a real human being who walked the dusty roads of northern

India about 2,500 years ago, at a time when India, like many other important regions around the world, was going through an important process of religious ferment. However, these historical facts don't tell us very much about what the Buddha did or about what he has meant to his followers in the Buddhist tradition.

To learn about the Buddha this way, we have to turn to stories Buddhists tell about the Buddha and learn to look at the Buddha through Buddhist eyes. To tell the story of the Buddha the way Buddhists tell it, we have to begin not with his birth, but with his previous births. The Buddhist tradition arose at a time when the doctrine of reincarnation was a basic assumption of Indian religious life. People assumed that human beings did not live just one life, and then go on to some kind of reckoning in an afterlife. They cycled around again and again in a continuous process of death and rebirth. This process was called in ancient India, *samsara*, which is, I'm happy to say, not to be confused with the perfume of the same name. Samsara is the name we give to the cycle of death and rebirth in classical India. The word "samsara" means "to wander from one life to the next, potentially without end."

You might ask yourselves as students of comparative religion, as I talk about the doctrine of samsara and about the life of the Buddha, how would you feel about the prospect of an endless cycle of life in this world, or possibly even in worlds that are not as pleasant as this one? In India, serious religious people began to think that samsara was not a particularly appealing idea. To my classes in Boston where I teach about the doctrine of samsara, usually at the end of the summer, September, early October, I say that the best way to recreate this feeling for themselves is to imagine that they are born again as Red Sox fans. My apologies to any of you who may be devoted Red Sox fans and don't like the drift of this analogy. Part of the law of living in Boston is the constant cycle of raising hopes that perhaps this will be the year when the magnificent event of a World Series victory may finally come to Boston. For one reason or another as happens not just in Boston but elsewhere in America too, these hopes seem inevitably to be dashed.

Well that feeling of disappointment, and disappointment that comes in a continuous cycle of hopes raised and hopes dashed, is a bit like the feeling that's associated with the doctrine of samsara. Samsara brings you back into this world with many possibilities and many hopes and dreams, but they're hopes and dreams that lead eventually to frustration, to death, and to rebirth again in another life. The great sages of India, like the Buddha and other sages in other religious traditions in India too, attempted to find a way out of the cycle of samsara. The idea was not to come back into this world and enjoy its pleasures once again, but to find a way to bring the cycle of samsara to a definitive conclusion.

People assumed in India that someone as important as the Buddha must have prepared for this possibility through an enormous number of previous lives, by studying under previous Buddhas and practicing all the virtues that would come to such glorious fruition in his final life as the Buddha Shakyamuni. The stories of the Buddha's previous lives are told in a body of texts that are known today as the *Jataka*, or the "Birth Tales." In their English translation, they occupy a number of hefty volumes. They would be a significant body of material if I lined them up in front of me here on my lectern.

Many of them are quite simple, almost childlike, and they sound best if they could be told with the lilting cadences of a child. I may not be able to recreate the right kind of childlike voice myself, but you can imagine what your favorite seven-year-old would sound like if you were telling the following story about a previous life of the Buddha:

Once upon a time there were three animals—a monkey, an elephant and a partridge—and they began to discuss which one of them was the oldest. The oldest was the one who would deserve special respect. The elephant pointed to a gigantic fig tree. (As you may know, the fig trees in South Asia are enormous. They're almost the size of cathedrals sometimes.) The elephant pointed to one of these massive trees and said, "I'm so old, I'm such an old elephant that when I was little I could walk over this tree and its leaves would barely touch my belly." The monkey said, "You may be pretty old, but when I was a little monkey I could reach up and pluck leaves from the topmost branches of that tree. That's how old I am compared to this tree." The partridge said that when he was young he ate a seed. The seed passed through his body, fell to the ground and grew up to become the tree. The elephant and the monkey bowed down and paid homage to the partridge.

The Jataka tale ends like other Jataka tales, with a common formula in the words Buddha, in the mouth of the Buddha, "And I the Buddha was that partridge." Technically, the being who appeared as that partridge was not actually the Buddha himself. He didn't become the Buddha until the life when he was born as Siddhartha Gautama. Buddhists refer to the partridge as a *bodhisattva*, or a "Buddha-to-be." You could also call a bodhisattva a "future Buddha," someone who is on the way to Buddha-hood in some future life. We'll see that Buddhists, in one way or another, whether they're little children telling a story about respect for elders or the most sophisticated monks and nuns, have to grapple with what it means for themselves to be bodhisattvas, people on the way to achieving Buddha-hood in some future life.

These Jataka tales teach moral lessons for everybody, not just for the people who expect to be Buddhas as Siddhartha Gautama himself was in this life. When Siddhartha Gautama's career as a bodhisattva was near its end, he was born as the son of King Shuddhodana and Queen Maya. As you can imagine, the story of his birth is full of miraculous signs. According to tradition the future Buddha sprang from his mother's side, took seven steps to the north and announced in a commanding voice "I am the best of the world. This is my last birth, and I will never be born again." That's rather unusual. It was rather unusual even for ancient India, for an event like that to take place.

It got the attention of his father, as you might well imagine. He called in the court sages and asked them to explain what these miraculous events actually meant. They saw that there were wheels inscribed on the palms of Siddhartha's hands and on the soles of his feet. They told his father that the child was destined to become a *chakravartin*, or a "turner of the wheel." The wheels could mean either that he would turn the wheel of conquest around India and become a great king, or he could turn the wheel of religious teaching and become a great sage. Either way, the wheel was the symbol of his status as a so-called *mahapurusha*, a great person.

The eight-spoked wheel of the Buddha's teaching is still used as a symbol of Buddhism on temples and in Buddhist sculpture today. Siddhartha's father tried to protect him from the suffering in the world in the hope that he would not choose what must have seemed to him to be the rather disreputable and unpleasant option of becoming a religious sage. For a while, according to the story, he was successful. Siddhartha was married. He had a child. He seemed to be content with his sheltered life in the palace, but one day he was riding in a park outside the palace and he saw four sights: a sick person, an old person, a corpse, and a wandering ascetic. According to the story, he was shocked by this vision of suffering. This came to him as something that he had simply not seen before, wasn't aware of in some emotional sense and it shocked him. It stopped him in his tracks. He decided to leave the palace to become an ascetic himself.

His process of leaving the palace, of shaving his head and giving away all of his possessions and taking up the robe and the begging ball of a wandering monk is another crucial event in the life of traditional Buddhists. It functions in many of the Buddhist countries of Southeast Asia as a coming of age ceremony. It's reenacted whenever a child or a young person or an older person leaves ordinary life to become a monk or a nun.

As a monk, Siddhartha did not immediately find much success according to the legends that are told about his life in Buddhist tradition. He joined a group of other ascetics and tried to confront the problems of old age and death by starving himself until he was nothing but skin and bones. There are some extraordinarily powerful Buddhist images of this phase in his life that show him with his eyes sunk deep in their sockets and veins standing out over the bones on his rib cage. It wasn't a particularly pleasant time for him. It didn't bring him the results he wanted, so he accepted a bowl of rice pudding from a young woman and withdrew into the style of life that Buddhists call a Middle Path.

The concept of the Middle Path is another one of these key ideas that grows right out of the legendary telling of the story of the Buddha. It colors every aspect of Buddhist life. The point is to avoid two extremes: the extreme of self-denial, like the self-denial that Siddhartha experienced when he almost starved himself to death, and the extreme of self-indulgence. These extremes apply not just to the way people live, as was true in the story about Siddhartha, but also to the way they think, especially to the way they think about themselves.

Buddhist philosophers constantly ask, "What do we mean when we use the word 'self'?" While they disagree exactly about the way they should formulate the answer to that question, the answers always involve the avoidance of two extremes. You can't affirm the self too much; attribute too much permanent identity to it. You also can't deny it too much because it needs to be taken seriously in order to pursue the religious life that someone like the Buddha was attempting to follow.

Once Siddhartha found the Middle Path, things began to move more quickly for him. He sat down under the tree that became known eventually as the *Bodhi Tree*, the tree of his awakening, and he fixed himself in meditation. He was tempted by Mara, who, in Buddhist tradition, is the personification of death and who first sent his daughters to seduce him and then sent his sons as an army to attack him. Usually people think that these armies were meant to scare Siddhartha and make him give up his meditation out of fear. I suppose that's the obvious interpretation of this story.

I think it's also fun every once in a while to just imagine a rather different scenario than the one that is traditionally presented. I sometimes think of these armies as being the vision of those young men who must have been the cronies, the friends of Siddhartha before he left the palace, left his life as a prince and took up the life of a religious teacher saying to him, "Come on, Siddhartha. Come on out and fight with us one more time. Just join our princely existence and fill yourself with that great rush of aggression that makes a princely life so satisfying and so full of energy." In any case, however you interpret it, whether you follow my fanciful interpretation or something that's a little bit more traditional, the Buddha, our future Buddha, Siddhartha, resisted these temptations and Mara was defeated.

You may perhaps know, if you know the tradition of Buddhist sculpture, that this is one of the most important iconic gestures for the statues of the Buddha. He's often shown in a gesture that is called the *bhumisparsha* gesture, the earth touching gesture, in which he reaches down, touches the earth, and the earth shakes to bear witness to the solidity of his meditation and of his resolve to defeat the forces of death and rebirth.

Once Mara had been defeated in the dark of the night, Siddhartha passed through several stages of meditation and finally understood what caused the suffering of the world and how he could bring it to a definitive end. This is the moment when we can properly call Siddhartha the Buddha, or the "Awakened One." You may have heard this word translated as the "Enlightened One." This is very common. It's common to speak about this moment in the Buddha's career as the moment of his enlightenment, but this is a misleading translation, I believe. Buddhists say that a Buddha is someone who has awakened from the dream of ignorance, and whose wisdom has blossomed like a flower. These days, we translate the word "Buddha" as the "Awakened One." I suppose it also would be fine to say that he's the one who has blossomed, but that just doesn't sound quite right in English, so we stick with the translation of this event as his awakening.

When Siddhartha became a Buddha, he also achieved the state or the goal that Buddhists call *nirvana*. There's a lot of confusion about nirvana, too. Buddhists don't make it any easier when they insist that only a Buddha can really know what nirvana is. For the rest of us, it may be enough simply to know what the word "nirvana" really means. Nirvana means "to extinguish" or "to blow out," like blowing out the flame of a candle. A Buddha is someone who not only has understood the causes of suffering, but he has extinguished them. He no longer suffers from the ignorance and desire that feed the fire of death and rebirth.

Tradition tells us that the Buddha was tempted to stay under the tree of his awakening and enjoy this experience of nirvana for himself, but instead he got up and he walked to Sarnath, a suburb that's on the outskirts of the city of Banaras, the great Hindu pilgrimage site on the bank of the Ganges River, and he taught about his awakening to a group of ascetics. This event is called in Buddhist tradition "the first turning of the wheel of the law," and it represents the beginning of Buddhist tradition. It's represented in Buddhist sculpture and Buddhist iconography with this wheel that was found also on the soles of the Buddha's feet and on the palms of his hands.

From this point on, the Buddha had a long and fruitful career, walking the roads of northern India, teaching to kings and peasants and merchants, converting monks and nuns and presiding over what became eventually a thriving monastic order. There are many wonderful stories about this phase in the Buddha's life, as you might well imagine. I said a few minutes ago that the Jataka tales would themselves occupy a large space on a bookshelf. That's even more true about the stories that are told about the Buddha's life.

I suppose each of us who studies Buddhism has a particular favorite, for its strange combination of psychological vividness and a dose of the miraculous. The story that appeals most to me is the story of a figure by the name of Angulimala, whose name means simply

"Garland of Fingers." It also has a heavy dose, I would have to say, of the bizarre. It's a very strange story, but it's one that tells quite a bit, I think, about the style of Buddhist tradition and perhaps, indeed, even about the style of the Buddha's own teaching.

When the story starts, Angulimala is a pious student. A classic A-student, occasionally we encounter them even in our own courses, eager to please his demanding teacher, and his classmates became so jealous about Angulimala's achievements that they told some scandalous stories about Angulimala and provoked the teacher to try to seek revenge against him. Angulimala went to his teacher and he asked how much he needed to pay for his final teaching. He really wanted to pay his teacher his final fee. The teacher said, "Your final fee, Angulimala, is to go out into the forest and bring me the severed fingers of a hundred people whom you have killed yourself." That was the fee. Very strange. Angulimala, the devoted student that he was, went out into the forest and attempted to follow his teacher's instructions. The word got around that this was going on. The king sent out a punitive expedition to capture Angulimala and bring him to justice.

Angulimala's mother heard that the king's soldiers were chasing Angulimala. She decided to go out and warn Angulimala so he could get away. By this time, the Buddha realized that Angulimala was so far gone that he would kill even his own mother to seize her fingers, so the Buddha went out to intercede. Then the story becomes interesting.

The Buddha is walking slowly through the forest and Angulimala comes running after him saying, "Stop, stop! I want your fingers!" The Buddha doesn't seem to be moving very fast, and yet no matter how fast Angulimala runs, the Buddha slips away from him. Angulimala says, "Stop, stop, you bald-headed old monk! Stop so that I can get your fingers!" The Buddha turns around and says, "Angulimala, I have stopped. Why don't you stop?" Angulimala says, "You haven't stopped. No matter how hard I run, you keep getting away from me." The Buddha says, "I have stopped all the causes of death and rebirth. Angulimala, why don't you stop?"

At this point Angulimala turns back into the student that he once was, and he throws himself down at the feet of the Buddha and, in tears, asks for his forgiveness and asks to be made a member of the monastic community. The Buddha initiates him into the monastery and makes him a monk.

It turns out that it's not quite so easy in Buddhist society to make such a radical change. When Angulimala went around and begged at the doors in the villages where he once had been such a terrifying presence, it wasn't a particularly easy thing for him to do. He eventually had to go through some very severe penances before he could finally come to realize the significance of the Buddha's teaching. Eventually he became one of the greatest monks of the tradition and an extraordinary example of a radical change in life that comes from seeing himself in a different way and renouncing all that he was to become a new person on the path to nirvana.

Another teaching tale that had tremendous significance in China and Japan is the story of Kashyapa. One day, according to this story, the Buddha was meeting with a group of monks. Instead of speaking to them, he held up a flower. Everyone in the group except for Kashyapa waited for an explanation. Kashyapa just smiled. The Buddha said, "There is a supreme teaching. Words cannot reach it. This supreme teaching I have just handed to Kashyapa."

Both these stories show us something about the Buddha and also something about the way Buddhist tradition has imagined this remarkable and important figure. Words have their place in Buddhism, but the Buddha's teaching can be conveyed just as well through gestures, through a smile, through a tilt of the head, or perhaps best of all through silence. The reason is that it's not just a teaching about words and concepts; it's a teaching about the way to live a serene and contemplative life. The Buddha taught this as much by his example as by his words.

At about the age of 80, the Buddha's teaching career finally came to an end. He gave his last teaching to the monks and lay down between two trees and passed gently from this life, never to be born again. Buddhists call this event his *parinirvana*, his complete nirvana, the fulfillment of everything he had set out to accomplish when he saw the four sights in the park outside his palace.

I said earlier that the Buddha's life did not begin with his birth. It's also true to say that his life did not end with his death. Before he died he told his disciples to take his body and cremate it, as they would cremate the body of a great king, and then to set up the relics of his cremation in large round shrines that were called *stupa* mounds. We could call them reliquary mounds, the mounds that would be used to house the relics of a great saint. Here people could come and pay homage to the Buddha as if he were still alive, even though he had passed on into his parinirvana and had ceased to be part of the cycle of death and rebirth.

There's much more that we could say about the Buddha's life. The traditions go on in a much more rich way than I'm able to suggest in just these few stories. You can see a few things from what I've said about the Buddha. You can see a few things that are important about the Buddha himself and also about the tradition that he helped set in motion.

First of all, the Buddha was a human being. He was not a god. Nor was he a manifestation of God. He was a human being who tried to confront the fundamental problems of suffering and death and bring them to a solution. He also did this in a tradition of Indian asceticism that had broad impact throughout the religious traditions of India, and he did it in a way that had extraordinary impact on the rest of the religious life of Asia, an impact that we will have a chance to explore much more deeply in the lectures that lie ahead.

Lecture Three
"All Is Suffering"

Scope:

When the Buddha left the Bodhi Tree, after he had experienced his awakening, he walked to a Deer Park in Sarnath, outside the city of Banaras; met a group of ascetics; and taught them about his awakening. This event is known as the first "turning of the wheel of Dharma [teaching]." Traditional accounts of the Buddha's teaching begin with the claim that "all is suffering." These words suggest that Buddhism is pessimistic and devalues human life. Buddhists say, however, that the tradition is not pessimistic but realistic. To see the world through Buddhist eyes, it is important to understand how the Buddha's understanding of suffering leads not to pessimism and discouragement but to a realistic assessment of life's difficulties and to a sense of liberation and peace.

Outline

I. The death of the Buddha left his followers with a difficult problem. During his life, the Buddha had been a focus of veneration and a source of authority. When the Buddha both died and left the realm of rebirth altogether, what was left to fill the void?

   A. Buddhists have typically given two answers to this question.

      1. For those who want to worship the Buddha, the Buddha left behind a Form Body, initially comprised of the relics left behind by the Buddha's cremation. Over time, any physical sign or representation of the Buddha came to play the same role, including objects the Buddha touched, places he visited, and images of the Buddha's form.

      2. For those who want to follow the Buddha's example, he left behind his Dharma, the teaching that expressed the content of his awakening and showed the way for others to achieve awakening for themselves.

   B. Out of this distinction between the Buddha's physical body and the body of his teaching came a theory of the two bodies of the Buddha. This theory is similar, in some respects, to the Christian speculation about the nature of Christ.

1. Christian theologians distinguish between the two natures of Christ: Christ is said to be both fully human and fully divine.
2. Buddhists say that the Buddha has two bodies: a physical or Form Body that arises and passes away like any other part of this changeable and transient world, and a Dharma Body that is eternal and does not change.
3. It is misleading, however, to think that the Buddha is divine with respect to either of these two bodies.

C. In this lecture, we begin our exploration of the Buddha's Dharma.

II. In the "Discourse on the Turning of the Wheel of Dharma" (*Dhammacakkappavattana Sutta*), the traditional summary of the Buddha's first sermon, the Buddha's teaching is summarized in Four Noble Truths.

A. The Four Noble Truths are:
1. The truth of suffering (*dukkha*).
2. The truth of the arising of suffering.
3. The truth of the cessation of suffering (also known as *nirvana* or *nibbana*).
4. The truth of the path that leads to the cessation of suffering.

B. The terms *dukkha* and *nibbana* are cited in Pali, the language of the earliest Buddhist scriptures. Pali is best understood as a vernacular form of Sanskrit, the classical language of India.

III. Some say that all of the Noble Truths are contained by implication in the seemingly simple claim that "all is suffering."

A. When people come to Buddhism for the first time, this statement often seems to be a barrier. It seems to mean that the Buddha (and, by implication, all Buddhists) was pessimistic. The first important intellectual challenge in the study of Buddhism is to understand how this simple statement about suffering leads not to pessimism but to a sense of liberation and peace.

B. Traditional sources say that "all is suffering" in one of three ways:

1. *Dukkha-dukkha* (suffering that is obviously suffering): Some things cause obvious physical or mental pain.
2. *Viparinama-dukkha* (suffering due to change): Even the most pleasurable things cause suffering when they pass away.
3. *Samkhara-dukkha* (suffering due to conditioned states): Pleasurable things can cause pain even in the midst of the pleasure, if the pleasure is based on an illusion about the nature of the object or about the nature of the self.

C. To make these abstractions more concrete, we can use the example of an automobile.
   1. A car causes *dukkha-dukkha* if you drive it into the back of a bus.
   2. A car causes *viparinama-dukkha* if you drive it through a New England winter and watch it disintegrate in the snow and salt.
   3. A car causes *samkhara-dukkha* if you think there is something in your sense of self that will be enhanced by attachment to the car.

D. The significance of these three kinds of suffering can be explained further by relating them to the three "marks" of existence.
   1. Everything is suffering.
   2. Everything is impermanent.
   3. Nothing has any self, or "all is no self" (*anatta*).

IV. What do Buddhists mean when they say that there is "no self"?

A. In traditional Buddhism, "no self" means that there is no permanent identity to continue from one moment to the next.

B. If there is no permanent identity, what makes up the human personality?
   1. The answer to this question is: five "aggregates," from material form (*rupa*) to consciousness (*vinnana*).
   2. These five aggregates are only momentary, but they group together to give the illusion of permanence, like the flow of a river or the flame of a candle.

C. If there is no self, what is reborn?
   1. The "stream" or "flame" of consciousness (*vi–ana*).

2. Because of the causal continuity between moments in the flame, it is possible to say that I am the "same" person from one moment to the next.

3. But when we look closely at the flame, we realize that it changes at every moment, and the idea that one moment is the same as another is nothing but an illusion.

V. Is the doctrine of suffering pessimistic?

A. The concept of no-self helps us understand why Buddhists do not consider the doctrine of suffering to be as negative as it seems.

1. From a Buddhist point of view, it is simply realistic to accept that the human personality and all of reality are constantly changing.

2. The cause of suffering is not the change itself, but the human desire to hold on to things and prevent them from changing.

B. When Buddhists look at the world through the lens of no-self, they do not approach it in a pessimistic way.

1. They understand that if everything changes, it is possible for everything to become new.

2. And if they accept the doctrine of suffering, it is possible to approach even the most difficult situations in life with a sense of lightness and freedom.

C. This doctrine also helps a person move forward on the path to nirvana.

1. If a Buddhist realizes that there is no permanent self, there is no longer any reason to be attached to all the things that bring someone back in the cycle of death and rebirth.

2. Just a hint of this realization is enough to start unraveling the chain of causes that bind people to samsara and get them moving toward nirvana.

Essential Reading:

Robinson and Johnson, *The Buddhist Religion*, ch. 2.

Rahula, *What the Buddha Taught*, ch. 2.

Supplementary Reading:

Strong, *The Experience of Buddhism*, ch. 3, sections 1–2.

Questions to Consider:

1. Why would it be attractive to think that there is no self?
2. Would this be a dangerous idea if it were understood in the wrong way?
3. How might Buddhists protect themselves against these dangers?

Lecture Three—Transcript
"All Is Suffering"

In our last lecture we discussed the life story of the Buddha. If we go back and we just place ourselves imaginatively back at that situation that the cycles of the Buddha faced right at the end of his life, we can see that the Buddha's death left his followers in a very difficult situation. During his life, the Buddha had been a focus of veneration and a source of authority. When the Buddha not only had died, but had left the realm of rebirth altogether, what was left to fill the void? Where could people turn to answer questions about Buddha's teaching, or to get some kind of advice to guide them in their practice?

Buddhists have typically given two answers to this question. For those who want to worship the Buddha, for whom veneration is really the key thing, the Buddha left behind what's called his "Form Body." This initially comprised the relics that were left behind by the Buddha's cremation. Over time, any physical sign or representation of the Buddha came to play the same role, including objects that the Buddha touched, places he visited, or statues or images, painted images in many cases, of the Buddha's form. On the other hand, for those who wanted to follow the Buddha's example, not simply to worship his physical presence, but actually to follow the example that he had provided for his community, he left behind his Dharma, the teaching that expressed the content of his awakening and showed the way for others to achieve awakening for themselves.

Out of this distinction between the Buddha's physical body and the body of his teaching came a theory about two bodies of the Buddha. This theory is similar in some respects to Christian speculation about the nature of Christ. As many of you know, I suspect, Christian theologians distinguish between the two natures of Christ. Christ is said to be simultaneously fully human and fully divine. Buddhists say that the Buddha has two bodies: the physical, or the Form Body that arises and passes away just like any other physical or material thing in this world, and the Dharma Body that is eternal and doesn't change.

It's misleading, I think, even though there is an apparent similarity between these two teachings about the Buddha and about Christ. It's misleading to draw the conclusion from this that the Buddha is divine with respect to either of these two bodies. The Form Body is a physical body and it passes away. The Dharma is simply the body of his teaching. It's not in any sense a body that can be equated with God or some form of divinity.

In this lecture what we want to do is to begin our exploration of the Buddha's Dharma, the Buddha's teaching, the teaching that he left behind for the monks and the nuns and the laypeople who attempted in one way or another to follow the example that led him eventually to nirvana. In an important traditional discourse that's called the "Discourse on the Turning of the Wheel of Dharma," the *Dhammacakkappavattana Sutta*, the traditional summary of the Buddha's first sermon, the Buddhist teaching is summarized in four noble truths—the four truths that I've already mentioned in my first lecture.

The first of these is the truth of suffering. The second is the truth of the arising of suffering. The third is the truth of the cessation of suffering that also can be equated with *nirvana*, or in the Pali language of Southeast Asia, *nibbana*. The fourth truth is the truth of the path that leads to the cessation of suffering.

I think we should note in passing here, even though this is not a course in any sense of Buddhist languages, that when you discuss these doctrines there are usually two languages that come into play in most Buddhist sources. We often hear of the suffering as *dukkha*, d-u-k-k-h-a, and *nirvana* as *nibbana,* n-i-b-b-a-n-a. These two words are in Pali, the language of the traditional scriptures of Southeast Asia. Pali is probably best understood, more or less, as a vernacular form of Sanskrit, which is the classical language of ancient India.

When I'm talking with my students about these two languages, I teach them that uncanny philological technique that you can use to go from the Sanskrit form of a word to a Pali form. All you have to do is stuff your mouth with Kleenex and try to pronounce the Sanskrit word, and the Pali will just simply fall out. We could try this together. If we were all together, we could try it together with the word nirvana, which is quite a precise word. If you stuff your mouth with Kleenex and try to say nirvana, you get something like the Pali word nibbana. In any case, all we have to be aware of is that there are a couple of languages at work here. You may very well, in some sources, want to discern the difference between the two.

Some people say that all of the four noble truths are contained by implication in the seemingly simple claim that all is suffering. The Pali phrase for this is *sabbam dukkham*, "all is suffering." I ask my students at Boston University every once in awhile to practice saying this with long and sour faces in the most dolorous way possible, partly to prepare for exam period when they may actually begin to feel that way, but also partly to just place themselves emotionally in a certain sense within that intellectual and affective problem of the concept of suffering in the Buddhist tradition. When people come to Buddhism for the first time, this simple claim, *sabbam dukkham*, all is suffering, often seems to be a real barrier to understanding. It seems to mean that the Buddha and, I suppose, by implication, all the Buddhists who have explored and expanded and passed on the teaching of the Buddha, were all pessimistic about the possibility of pleasure and happiness in human life.

The first important intellectual challenge for us, as we begin to dig more deeply into the serious aspects of Buddhist teaching, is to understand how this simple statement about suffering doesn't really lead to pessimism, but to a sense of liberation and peace, to a sense of quiet and of happiness and nirvana. The best way to do this is to explore some of the more sophisticated accounts of suffering in Buddhist literature, where we see that *dukkha*, suffering, is interpreted not just one way, but in three ways that lead more deeply and in a more sophisticated way into the significance of the concept.

The first form of suffering is pretty obvious. It's called *dukkha-dukkha*, the suffering that is obviously suffering, suffering that is physical pain or emotional pain, when you feel something that simply hurts you and its suffering is undeniable. The second kind of suffering is called *viparinama-dukkha*. It's the suffering that's due to change. It comes when even the most pleasurable things cause suffering when they pass away. Often they cause suffering in direct relationship to the degree of attachment that you invest in them. If you have something that you really like and that you're really attached to—a physical object, a person, a kind of experience—and all of a sudden it slips away from you, that feeling of losing it is a painful experience. That's the pain that Buddhists refer to as *viparinama-dukkha*, the suffering due to change.

The final form of suffering, the third form, is called *samkhara-dukkha*, and it's difficult to explain. I think sometimes I'm not sure I really understand it. Buddhist sources say sometimes that *samkhara-dukkha* is as difficult to perceive as an eyelash held in the palm of your hand. For sages, it is as palpable and as painful as the same eyelash stuck in your eye. *Samkhara-dukkha* means simply suffering due to conditioned states. It seems to refer to pleasurable things that can cause pain, even in the midst of their pleasure, if the pleasure is based on some kind of an illusion about the nature of the object, or about the nature of your own self. It's experiencing the object.

When I work with students on these three types of suffering, I try to build parables. That's a classic Buddhist activity. The Buddha himself taught in parables. Often the parables that we build for ourselves are instinctively in a certain way very similar to the parables that were used in the Buddhist tradition itself. My first and most basic parable is the parable of the automobile, the parable of a car.

We teach in Boston on a very busy street. Commonwealth Avenue runs right by our classroom building. I can stroll over to the window and take a look out the window and imagine that I'm seeing someone going by in a very beautiful sports car on a wonderful fall day, top down and music blaring on the sound system, roaring down Commonwealth Avenue rejoicing in the pleasure of the day and in the surge of pleasure that comes from being in a great car.

The guy in the car, it's always a guy. I suppose that's discriminatory in some profoundly disturbing way, but let's just imagine that this is a young man who's driving this automobile down the street. He turns around, waves to his girlfriend on the side of the road, and runs into the back of a big MBTA bus. The pain that he feels when the car hits the back of the bus I think we can say is dukkha-dukkha. Something painful occurs. We won't speculate about how it feels in his body, but we know that that's a painful thing. That's dukkha-dukkha.

The second kind of dukkha would come, I suppose for the same person who takes the car through a New England winter, when there's snow on the road and there are lots of potholes and the car begins to get beaten up. Perhaps it's vandalized. Whatever pleasure that car once brought begins to slip away and turn into something that is much closer to frustration and pain as the beautiful object begins to disintegrate. That's the second kind of suffering. It's pretty easy. You don't need to really build an elaborate parable to try to explain this.

The third kind of suffering is a little more problematic, but I think not too far-fetched or too difficult to imagine. Take a look at the guy, our imaginary figure, driving this imaginary car down a street that exists also in our imaginations together. Ask ourselves, as he surges along feeling the pleasure of this automobile, the pleasure of this day, feeling somehow that his self has been expansively affirmed by this extraordinary surge of energy that he's part of in the New England landscape, is he really happy? That's the question. We never put this to a vote in our class, but we talk about it often. Is he really happy? The question that lurks in the back of your mind always is whether he has created some kind of an illusory construct of himself that's connected with that mass of metal and rubber and leather, whatever it is that makes up this automobile. It has created an illusion for himself of who he is that, in the end, will cause him pain when the illusion begins to slip away.

The third form of suffering has to do with this kind of an illusion, some sort of an illusory sense of ourselves that we create out of the objects that we use to populate our world, or the experiences that we seek to try to develop ourselves in some way into an image of what we would like to be. Often times these illusions are extremely pleasurable, but if they don't match the reality of our lives and the reality of our situation, Buddhists will say that we're suffering a form of pain; that there's a subtle feeling of pain even in the midst of the pleasure.

Another story that I tell in the same setting that I think perhaps comes a little closer to the depth of Buddhist experience has to do not so much with an automobile, but with a self, with a person. We know that we can be in relationships often with other people that are directly painful. There's no need to really talk about those. I suppose people can be physically violent to us or abusive in ways that cause dukkha-dukkha. They also can cause pain to us when relationships change and people cease to be the kind of people that they once were for us, and the people that we were attached to begin to slip away and become something else. Sometimes the most painful kinds of human relationships are ones, not so much where someone is abusive to us in any sort of direct way or even when they cease to be the kind of people that we once thought they were, but when we impose on them, or they impose on us, illusions that expect us to be something other than what they are.

This I think is a particular concern for students in many of my classes. They've all left home fairly recently, in many cases. They are often freshmen or sophomores and they're well aware that their parents have images and expectations of them that are difficult for them to live up to, and they know very well how painful those are and how difficult it is for them to negotiate, in some way, some space for their own emerging reality as human beings. The painfulness of that situation comes directly out of that gap between illusion and reality, between expectations that we have of others and expectations that we have of ourselves, and the reality of what they are and of what we are for ourselves.

Suffering for Buddhists has to do, in the end, with this kind of illusion—an illusion that there's a physical object out there that will feed us in some emotional way and give us satisfaction that we would not be able to acquire some other way, or illusions about others and about ourselves. Illusions that, in the end, are disappointed.

If this is what suffering means, if this is where Buddhists want to take us with this concept, what do they really mean by self? What do they mean when they talk about the personality? Clearly, no matter how we work into the concept of suffering, it comes back in the end to a sense of misconception, illusion, however we want to describe it, about the nature of our own personality. If this is really the key issue, what do Buddhists think the personality is?

The key concept in Buddhist approaches to the nature of the self is the concept of no-self. Buddhists insist, in the end, when you look at the human personality and you look at the flow of reality around us, that there is no permanent identity that endures for one moment to the next. Then distill this concept into a single phrase, no-self, "*anatta*" in Pali, "*anatman*" in Sanskrit. What do they mean when they say there is no-self? In traditional Buddhism, no-self means that there's simply no permanent identity that endures from one moment to the next. If there is no permanent identity, what is it then that makes up this massive phenomena that we associate with our physical and cognitive presence in the world?

The answer to this question, in classic Buddhist doctrine, is five aggregates, five things leading from material form, our physical nature, up to the aggregate of our consciousness. These five aggregates are only momentary, but they group together. They come together in bundles to give us the illusion of some kind of permanence like the flow of a river or like the burning of a candle flame. Buddhists think of the personality as if it were simply a constant flow, a stream of phenomena that moves and changes and evolves from one moment to the next, and burns like the flame of a fire as experiences are drawn into the fire, consumed, and then the fire moves on to some other kind of experience to feed itself and burn up.

A classic question that Buddhists ask when they reach this stage in the discussion of the self has to do with the doctrine of no-self. If there is no-self, if the self that we observe and we attribute so much reality to is nothing but a stream, nothing but a fire burning through a stream of experiences, what is it that is reborn? What moves from one life to the next? The answer to this question, in classic Buddhist thought, is the stream or flame of consciousness itself. When a death occurs in this world and a bundle of aggregates—the momentary phenomena that make up a personality—begins to exhaust itself, the consciousness, the last moment of consciousness, gives rise to another moment of consciousness elsewhere that begins to take form as a new personality. It's neither the same nor different from the personality that was there before. It's simply a causal connection that leads from one moment to the next, as the personality constantly changes.

Because of the causal continuity between moments in the flame, if we want to state this doctrine in a precise form, it's possible to say that I am the same person from one moment to the next. We would put the word "same" here in quotation marks. It's just the causal connection that makes you the same. When we look closely at the flame, we realize that it changes at every moment. The idea that one moment is the same as another is nothing but an illusion. That's the classic Buddhist doctrine of no-self: a stream of causes like a river—like a candle flame—that burns, leaving each moment behind as a new moment comes into existence.

It's always interesting, I'd have to say, to discuss this doctrine with Buddhists who work and live within this vision of the world, especially when you encounter the doctrine of transmigration itself. I think all of us who study Buddhism have had the experience of going to India, or going to some other portion of Asia, perhaps to Tibet or to Southeast Asia, and imagining that we're finally going to get an answer to the question that always had occurred to us and always puzzled us when we first encountered the tradition. What do you really believe about the doctrine of transmigration? Do you really believe it?

I remember asking, in my naiveté, asking that question of a Tibetan monk that I knew once in Boston who came to Boston as the recognized reincarnation of a great monk from a previous generation in eastern Tibet. I took him aside one day and said, "Okay, Tulku-la, there's nobody else listening, we can close all the windows and take the telephone off the hook so that no one will overhear our conversation. Tell me what it was like to be a monk in eastern Tibet in your previous incarnation." He just laughed, as Buddhists often do, just smiled at me and said, "David, I can't even remember what I had for breakfast, let alone what I did in my previous life."

I took from that not just a sneaky way of avoiding the question, it probably was true that he didn't really remember very much of his previous life, but also a rather subtle and effective reminder of something important about the Buddhist tradition. There's really nothing more mysterious about rebirth, the passing from one life to another, than there is in our passing from one moment to another. Even in our own experience, we constantly change. The person who is here today is a very different person than the one who was here yesterday. To grasp the reality of ourselves, to come to terms with it in some deep way, we have to come to terms with that changeable aspect of our own experience, that even in this moment, everything that we experience is flowing through us and constantly changing. The people who started out a minute ago, 10 minutes ago, 20 minutes ago, whenever it was, talking about the Buddhist Dharma, have now become something completely different.

The question we have to ask about this doctrine is really the question we began with. Is this doctrine of suffering and of no-self, because the doctrine of no-self is really part of the doctrine of suffering, is it pessimistic? Is it as negative as it initially seems? I think that the concept of no-self helps us understand why Buddhists themselves do not consider the doctrine of suffering to be particularly pessimistic. From a Buddhist point of view, it's simply realistic. It's simply an act, a real encounter with the nature of reality to accept that the human personality and everything around it is constantly changing.

The cause of suffering is not really the change itself, but the human desire to hold onto things and prevent them from changing.

When Buddhists look at the world through the lens of no-self, they don't really approach it in a particularly pessimistic way. They understand that if everything changes, it's possible for everything to become new. If they accept the doctrine of suffering, it's possible to approach even the most difficult situations in life with a sense of lightness, of buoyancy and freedom. Truthfully, when we live and work in Buddhist cultures or encounter Buddhist people in simple and unpretentious settings, we encounter people who are not particularly oppressed by an oppressive—or by a pessimistic—difficult, sad vision of the world. Even though it's based on this doctrine of the impermanence of all things, there's a sense of buoyancy and lightness.

People are quick to laugh and quick to let go of things that are painful. Why? Because everything changes. Everything is impermanent. In the end, there's nothing to hold onto that will cause us any pain. This doctrine, the doctrine of no-self, also helps a person move forward on the path to nirvana. If a Buddhist realizes that there is no person—permanent self—if there's no eternal, enduring entity in the personality that you have to hold on to, then there's no longer any reason to be attached to all the things that bring someone back into the cycle of death and rebirth.

Just a hint of this realization, this awareness of no-self, is enough to start unraveling the chain of causes and conditions that fuel the cycle of reincarnation. By unraveling this chain, it's possible to take a step forward on the path that will lead a person eventually to the experience of nirvana. I think you'd have to say—just from this very brief encounter with the Buddha's teaching—that the heart of it really rests in two key ideas. The idea first of all, that everything is impermanent, constantly in a state of change, and the idea that nothing has any permanent identity that we need to hold on to in order to satisfy our craving for experience in this world. If we can realize that, if we can come to that kind of understanding, we've taken a step forward on the path toward nirvana.

Lecture Four
The Path to Nirvana

Scope:

After presenting the truth of suffering, the Buddha went on to describe the origin of suffering, the cessation of suffering, and the path that leads to the cessation of suffering. Buddhists refer to the cessation of suffering as *nirvana*, literally, the "blowing out" of desire. Like the concept of suffering, nirvana at first seems extremely pessimistic. In some respects, this is inescapable. Nirvana marks the definitive end of the cycle of rebirth. But nirvana does not need to be viewed in a negative way, especially when it is understood as a realization that infuses and enlivens the Buddha's experience from the time of his awakening to the moment of his death.

Outline

I. The Second Noble Truth is the truth of the origin of suffering.

   A. The origin of suffering is explained by a causal sequence known as the twelve-fold chain of dependent arising (*paticca-samuppada*).

   B. The most important links in this chain show a process that leads from ignorance to birth.
   1. Ignorance leads to desire.
   2. Desire leads to birth.

   C. To understand what Buddhists have in mind when they make this series of connections, you might take a glossy advertisement and ask what kinds of illusions it fosters, what kinds of desires it is meant to arouse, and what comes into being as a result of those desires. Most of these illusions are quite benign, but they feed a process that, for Buddhists, leads to more death and rebirth.

   D. The most fundamental form of ignorance is that "I" constitutes a permanent ego that needs to be fed by new and desirable experiences or new and desirable objects.

II. The Third Noble Truth is the truth of cessation or nirvana.

   A. When someone begins to cultivate an awareness of no-self and strips away the desires that feed the fire of samsara, it is possible eventually for the fire of samsara to burn out.

1. This is not easy, and it may take many lifetimes.
2. But it is possible for anyone to achieve the same cessation of samsara that was experienced by the Buddha himself.

B. This cessation is known by the name nirvana (*Pali nibbana*).
   1. Nirvana means to "blow out," as if one were extinguishing the flame of a candle.
   2. Nirvana can be understood as the "blowing out" of desire, the "blowing out" of ignorance, or the "blowing out" of life itself, if life is understood as the constant cycle of death and rebirth.
   3. Nirvana comes at two moments: at the moment of awakening, when the Buddha understood that he was no longer adding fuel to the fire of his personality, and at the moment of *parinirvana*, when the fire of his personality finally flickered out.
   4. These two moments are called "nirvana with residues" and "nirvana without residues."

C. Like the concept of suffering, nirvana seems at first to be quite negative. Why do Buddhists find it so attractive?
   1. The concept of nirvana forces us to take seriously the negative Indian evaluation of samsara. If samsara really is something to be avoided, then the most positive thing to do about samsara is simply to negate it, to bring it to an end. Nirvana is this negation.
   2. This view of nirvana as cessation is quite different from a Jewish or Christian concept of the goal of life. According to Jewish and Christian tradition, God created the world out of nothing. You could say that God once faced "nothing" and made something come to be. The Buddha did the opposite. He faced a situation in which death and rebirth had been going on for time without beginning, and he found a way to bring his part of this cycle to an end.

3. Another way to explain the appeal of nirvana is to understand that the experience of nirvana is not limited to the moment of the Buddha's death. The Buddha also experienced nirvana at the moment of his awakening, when he knew that he was no longer bound by the ignorance and desire that fuel samsara.

   a. When nirvana is understood in this way, it is not just the cessation of life. It is a quality of mind or a state of being that characterizes the Buddha's life in the 40 years between his awakening and his parinirvana.

   b. During this time, the Buddha exemplified many characteristics that we would consider quite positive: He was peaceful, wise, unattached, and free. We could imagine that he also was able to act with a certain spontaneity and clarity of mind, perhaps even with a certain amount of compassion for the suffering of others.

III. The Fourth Noble Truth is the truth of the path.

   A. The path to nirvana is divided into eight categories: right understanding, right thought, right speech, right action, right livelihood, right effort, right mindfulness, and right concentration.

   B. The logic of the path is more clear, however, if we reduce these eight categories to three: *sila*, or moral conduct; *samadhi*, or mental concentration; and *pa–a*, or wisdom. These three categories give us a concise summary of basic Buddhist practice.

   1. Buddhist laypeople observe five moral precepts (*sila*): no killing, no stealing, no lying, no abuse of sex, and no drinking of intoxicants.

   2. Monks observe five more, including the restrictions that they cannot eat after noon, cannot sleep on soft beds, and cannot handle gold or silver.

   3. Buddhist practitioners engage in mental concentration (*samadhi*) to focus and clarify the mind.

   4. They also cultivate wisdom (*panna*), or the understanding of no-self.

   C. These three modes of discipline are meant to avoid the bad *karma* (or "action") that leads to difficult and dangerous forms of rebirth. They also are meant to cultivate the qualities of wisdom and detachment that eventually led to the Buddha's experience of awakening.

Essential Reading:

Strong, *The Experience of Buddhism*, ch. 3, sections 3–6.

Supplementary Reading:

Rahula, *What the Buddha Taught*, chs. 3 ff.

Questions to Consider:

1. Western religious traditions, such as Judaism and Christianity, emphasize the idea of God the creator. According to the story of creation, God once looked out on a formless void (or on nothing) and made something come into being. This has produced a preference for ideas of creativity and being and a suspicion of cessation and non-being. Is there a place in Western religions for an experience of "cessation?" Would it be better if there were?

2. The Buddhist path is meant to lead a person to nirvana and to stop the cycle of rebirth. How is the path structured to help Buddhists achieve this goal? How would the Buddhist path change a person's life even if he or she did not have the goal of nirvana in mind?

Lecture Four—Transcript
The Path to Nirvana

In our last lecture, we began our study of the Buddhist teaching of the Buddhist Dharma by talking about the first of the four noble truths. It was the truth of suffering. We talked a bit about one of the classic interpretive problems that are connected with this doctrine, the problem that we simply call problem of pessimism. It seems on the face of it to be pretty pessimistic. We came to the conclusion at the end of that discussion that it wasn't exactly pessimistic. From a Buddhist point of view, it's simply realistic. It leads to a certain quality of buoyancy and lightness and freedom in relation to a lot of the things that otherwise make people rather fearful and concerned about letting go of many of the pleasurable and valuable and lovely things about experiencing this life.

In this lecture, we want to move on from that discussion of the first noble truth to talk about the other three, the final three categories or topics of discussion that help us get some sort of a sense of the basic outline of Buddhist teaching, teaching out of which so much of the rest of the tradition eventually evolved.

Let's begin with the second noble truth, which is the truth of the origin of suffering. It's said in the classic accounts of the Buddha's life that when he was under the tree of his awakening he understood not just that everything was suffering, but that everything had an origin. It came from a certain cause and could lead eventually to an experience of freedom from the suffering that afflicts so many aspects of human life. The origin of suffering is explained in classic Buddhist doctrine by a causal sequence that's known as the twelve-fold chain of dependent arising. The Pali word for this chain is the longest Pali word that we'll encounter in our study of this aspect of the tradition. It's called *paticca-samuppada*.

If we were all together in a classroom I'd get you to repeat that after me, but there's something about the barrier of this technology that seems to make that impossible. I'll say it one more time and you can roll it off your own tongues, *paticca-samuppada*. The "T" is particularly nice actually. You make that sound by putting the tip of your tongue in the roof of your mouth, *paticca-samuppada*, dependent co-arising. Things come into existence by depending on a whole bunch of causes. That's basically what that concept means.

We could go through 12 of the links in the chain, and it would be somewhat bewildering. I've always found the chain to be a little bit confusing, especially in some of the links, because it seems historically that it really is a combination of two attempts to explain the origin of suffering that have been cemented together. I think it's more valuable to just single out the key links that seem to, in one way or another, express for us the view of the world that is encapsulated in this vision of the origin of suffering.

The first link that's important is the link that leads from ignorance to desire. The idea here is that if you have a misconception about the nature of things, out of that misconception can come some sort of a desire for those things. Ignorance is really the start of the chain. Out of the desire comes birth. You have a process here where ignorance leads to some kind of desire or thirst for some particularly desirable object, and then out of that desire we try in one way or another to bring that object into being. Ignorance is the initial cause that fuels the chain of conditions that brings us back into the cycle of samsara.

To understand what Buddhists have in mind when they make this series of connections, one way to work with it might be to imagine something like a glossy advertisement. Simply put ourselves in the world of marketing and imagine an advertisement that creates an image for ourselves as fantastic as that may be of some extraordinarily desirable thing or experience or trip or whatever that may be. Ask what kinds of illusions it fosters, what kinds of desires it's meant to arouse, and what comes into being as a result of all of those desires. Most of those illusions for the large body of our experiences are pretty benign, but they feed a process that for Buddhists leads eventually to more of the cycle of death and rebirth. This is the engine, as it were, that fuels the cycle of samsara.

The most fundamental form of ignorance is not just ignorance about physical things that are outside ourselves, but ignorance about the self in the form that we just discussed in the last lecture. The ignorance that I, as a person, constitute some kind of permanent ego that needs to be fed by new and desirable experiences or new and desirable possessions. That explains for us the origin of suffering. It's a very simple picture really. It's not one that is difficult to grasp. It pins principal responsibility for the energy of samsara on ignorance, some kind of misconception about the nature of the world, and the nature of the self.

The third noble truth, truth of the cessation of suffering, the truth of *nirvana* or *nibanna*, tells us that when someone begins to cultivate an awareness of no-self, begins to understand that in some kind of deep and experiential way, and begins to strip away the desires that feed the fire of this cycle, it's possible eventually for the fire of samsara to burn out. This obviously is not easy in Buddhist experience, but it is possible for anyone to achieve the same cessation of samsara that was experienced by the Buddha himself, even though it may take many lifetimes.

It's usually understood in Southeast Asia that nirvana doesn't come particularly easily. It's something that takes many, many lifetimes to achieve and happens very rarely. This cessation is known by the name nirvana, which means simply to blow out as if one were extinguishing the flame of a candle. Nirvana can be understood perhaps as the blowing out of desire. That's one way to read the word. It also could be the blowing out of ignorance. If you wanted to take a really hard interpretation of the concept, you could see it as the blowing out of life itself if you think of life as this repetitive cycle of death and rebirth.

Nirvana comes at two moments: classically in the discussion of the Buddha's life, at the moment of his awakening when he understood that he was no longer adding fuel to the fire that fed his personality, and at the moment of his *parinirvana*, at his death when the fire of the personality finally flickered out. Technically, in the terminology of classic Buddhist thought, these two moments are called nirvana with residues and nirvana without residues.

Like the concept of suffering, we're here once again in this problematic world of negativity. It seems on the face of it that the concept of nirvana is very negative and difficult for us anyway as Western people to put any kind of positive spin on. I have often encountered, sometimes in more vocal ways than others, people who react pretty negatively to the concept of nirvana as I have just laid it out for you here. One particularly vocal and wonderful group of human beings once challenged me about this concept when I was lecturing at the Navy War College in Newport, Rhode Island. I don't often go down to speak to Navy officers about issues like non-violence and nirvana. By some marvelous good fortune, perhaps by the influence of something that I've done in a past life, whatever it was, it caused me to be invited to go and speak to them about all of this.

I'd weighed out the concept of nirvana as I always do. The concept of nirvana means literally to blow out or extinguish the desire that causes this cycle of death and rebirth. And one fairly taut and fit and obviously intelligent man raised his hand and he said, "Professor, I've got to tell you that this is the only time I have ever heard the concept of flame out spoken of as being a positive concept." I guess, what little I know about the life of a pilot on an aircraft carrier, flame out is not a particularly good idea. But here in this case flame out is good.

In the case of nirvana, it's good to have the fire of samsara, of desire and ignorance, eventually burn out. It does pose a problem for us again. What are we to make in such a negative image of the goal of human life? Here we have a religious tradition where the ultimate goal of human existence is to allow the fire that fuels this creative process of life after life eventually to extinguish itself. How can we understand that? How can we make sense of this idea? I think that the first thing that you have to say about this is that the concept of nirvana forces us to take seriously the negative Indian evaluation of samsara. I think very often for Western people, when we encounter the Indian doctrine of death and rebirth, our first impulse emotionally, if not intellectually, is to say, "It's not such a bad idea. I wouldn't mind coming back a few times here, maybe not a million times, but at least a few times because there are some things that I've let go in this life that I wouldn't mind having a chance to pick up again. You may not like it in traditional Buddhism, but for me it looks like a pretty appealing thing."

Not so in this tradition. The concept of nirvana shows us that, in classic Indian Buddhism, the cycle of samsara is something that is best when it simply stops. Nirvana for us is an image simply of cessation. It forces us to look seriously in the Buddhist tradition at all the different ways in which Buddhists are telling us that to cease activity is the goal of human life. It involves a major shift in our own imagination and in our own sense of what's valuable and important about human experience.

I often explore this with students by setting up a comparison and a contrast between this aspect of Buddhism and Judaism or Christianity. According to Jewish and Christian tradition, there is a story told about the process of creation in which God in some fashion once looked out and saw that there was nothing. Call it perhaps primordial chaos. Call it if you want simply nothing as in the classic Christian doctrine of creation *ex nihilo*, creation out of nothing. God made something come into being. That was that primordial act of creativity in which God took nothing and made something come to be. I think you'd agree with me that for Christian people or for Jewish people or for others who may in one way or another live in the context of this great story of creation, our job as people who, in one way or another, are acting or mirroring the image of God, is to face the chaos of our lives, the nothing of our experience and make something marvelously creative come into existence out of the nothing that we encounter in our world.

We put a tremendous value on creativity and the ability especially to create something out of nothing. The Buddhist tradition, interestingly enough, has exactly the opposite image of human life. The Buddha is a person who looked out in his world, beginning perhaps with the four sights that he saw when he took his trip through the park as a young man, certainly later in his experience as well, and he saw that life had been going on from beginning less time. Samsara has no beginning in the Indian tradition—they'd been going on from beginning less time.

He discovered a way in his own experience to make some of that stop. Instead of creating something out of nothing, he, as it were, created nothing out of something. That model is a model that he bequeaths to us. He gives to us to follow, if we place ourselves in his tradition and follow his example. The first thing to say about the apparent negativity in the concept of nirvana is that it's there and it's important. It forces us to take seriously an aspect of the Indian valuation of the cycle of samsara that we might not be inclined to take seriously when we first encounter it.

The second thing to say about nirvana that also is important, I think, and helps us understand why the concept is so immensely appealing to Buddhists, is that the experience of nirvana is not just limited to the moment of the Buddha's death. It doesn't just name that time when he himself as a personality simply ceased to exist. The Buddha also experienced nirvana at the moment of his awakening when he knew that he was no longer bound by ignorance and desire and no longer was enmeshed in the cycle of samsara. When we understand the concept this way, and when we encounter the experience this way, we can see that nirvana for Buddhists is not just the cessation of life. He lived for 40 years between that first moment of nirvana and the moment of his parinirvana.

Nirvana is a quality of mind or a state of being that characterizes the Buddha's life for the whole 40-year period between his awakening and his death. That period represents, you might say, the ultimate achievement of human life in Buddhist tradition. What does it look like? How would we characterize it for ourselves? Certainly, the images that we have of the Buddha tell us that he was peaceful. He was very calm. Lots of his illusions and fears and concerns and hopes and desires had slipped away. He also was wise. He was able to see reality for what it was, to understand it and respond to it in its reality. He was unattached. There was nothing that bound him. He was free.

One of the words for nirvana that's very commonly used in the Buddhist tradition is the Indian word for freedom, for liberation. We're talking here about a tradition in a sense of radical freedom, of detachment from the things that tie you to this world and drive the cycle of suffering. I think it's also possible for us to imagine that he was able out of this nirvana to act with a certain quality of spontaneity, clarity of mind. Perhaps even with a certain amount of compassion and attentiveness to the suffering of others. We can begin to build for ourselves an image that goes beyond simply the image of extinction that pictures what's valuable and wonderful about the life of a Buddhist sage. Nirvana is indeed the cessation of samsara, but also, in many respects for Buddhists, is the perfect fruition of these qualities of calm, wisdom, and freedom that can characterize fulfilling human life.

If that's what nirvana is, how do you get it? What's the path that leads to nirvana? This takes us to the fourth and last of the four noble truths, the path to the cessation of suffering. Classic accounts of the path are divided into eight categories: right understanding, right thought, right speech, right action, right livelihood, right effort, right mindfulness, and right concentration. I've always found that the eight categories somewhat mystify my mind. I'd rather find some way to simplify them or at least group them in a way that would tell me a bit about the logic of their relationship. I'm in the habit of grouping this system of eight together in a system of three that allows us to see a bit how Buddhists practice and organize their behavior in a way that will lead them eventually to the experience of nirvana. These three categories are *sila*, moral conduct; *samadhi*, or mental concentration; and *panna*, or wisdom. These categories give us what I think is a pretty good and concise summary of Buddhist practice, what it means to follow in the footsteps of the Buddha.

Let me just summarize them and give you a sense about how they function in Buddhist experience. Buddhist laypeople are expected to observe five moral precepts: no killing, no stealing, no lying, no abusing sex, and no drinking intoxicants—the five basic moral prohibitions of Buddhist life. Monks are expected to observe five more, including, I won't list all five, but including restrictions that they cannot eat after noon. They can't sleep on soft beds, and they can't handle gold and silver. The restriction on soft beds has always been the one that has both puzzled and amused me the most, especially when I encounter Buddhist monks from a particularly ascetic tradition.

I once was involved in the administration of a center in Harvard that had many visitors coming from religious traditions of Asia. One day we invited into the center a remarkably ascetic and well-organized monk from Thailand. We showed him his room, the room that we had set up for him to stay in. Actually I was kind of embarrassed. It was a pretty harsh and austere setting. The room itself didn't have any decoration on the walls, and the bed that we gave him had a very thin foam rubber pad that had probably not been changed in about, I'd say, 15 or 20 years. It had become petrified so that it was probably not much better than sleeping on a piece of stone. The monk took one look at this and thought that this was far too comfortable. He took the foam rubber pad off the bed, put it on the floor and slept on the chain link frame of the bed itself. I was taught one more important lesson about the austerity of Buddhist practice.

These are restrictions that are taken seriously and are important in the evolution of the tradition as a whole. They all belong in that larger category of *sila*, moral precepts, prohibitions against certain kinds of behavior that might lead to unhealthful or unhealthy states of mind.

The second category into which we would group the practice of the path is the category of mental concentration. This is the category that I would identify with what we would call Buddhist meditation. The cultivation of the mind that allows you to focus on your experience and to become calm in such a way that you can see the world clearly for what it is. Our course here is obviously not meant to be a course in meditation. If you wanted to be instructed in meditation, I'm sure that there're some other more wonderful ways for you to go about doing this. It would be crazy for me not to tell you how you could start.

Let's just imagine for ourselves what basic Buddhist meditation might be like. You would sit in a comfortable and stable way, in a chair perhaps, if that's the best place for you. If you can get your legs into a cross-legged position so that you can sit stably on the floor—that would be wonderful, too. You would keep your back straight, fold your hands in front of you—one hand over the other with your thumbs just touching—and allow your body to relax. Allow the tension in your body just to begin to slip away from your head down to your neck, down to your shoulders, down through the rest of your body.

Then breathe in a natural way and focus on the movement of your breath, counting with each breath until you reach the number 10, and then going back and counting again from one. As you do this, allow your attention to slip away from your busy, buzzing old head down into the pit of your stomach where your breathing center is. As my old yoga teacher in India used to say, just let the thoughts slip out of your head like dirty water out of a bathtub, and allow the mind to become calm. This is sometimes referred to as mindfulness of breathing. It's the mindfulness of the breath that is really the foundation of Buddhist meditation. Out of this, all other meditations grow. It's a marvelous way to bring you to a state of calm, a state that Buddhists refer to as *samadhi*, mental concentration. This is really the heart of the practice, Buddhist meditation.

The third category I want to mention, that has to do with the practice of the path, is the cultivation of wisdom. These three categories: moral precepts, mental concentration, and the cultivation of wisdom. What does it mean to be wise in the Buddhist tradition? To understand no-self really, to understand that basic insight into the nature of the world and the nature of the self. This could be understood in a far more sophisticated way than what we've been able to talk about here ourselves. It's really through this door that the whole tradition of Buddhist philosophy comes to greet us. Wisdom is cultivated often in many traditions through a very sophisticated process of philosophical study.

I could give you a capsule summary of that, I suppose. In a way, it might be better for me to tell you a story rather than to attempt to teach you philosophy—tell you a story about a great philosopher and an encounter that taught me a great deal, not just about the intellectual movement of the Buddhist philosophical tradition, but about the feeling that it brings to life. I once was asked to introduce the Dalai Lama to a group of people at Harvard, and get him going on a lecture that had to do with the Buddhist idea of selfhood. I spoke a bit about how important it was for us to greet him and then turn things over to him. He began to talk about the Buddhist concept of self by telling us how important it was for us to be compassionate to others. He began, in other words, by saying that we should be concerned about other people in a very simple way. That was, as it were, the starting point of his philosophical investigation of the nature of the self.

Then he said, "Those of you who have studied some Buddhism realize that it's perhaps a bit naïve to say that I should be concerned about someone else, because I know that I have no self, and others have no self either. So what do we mean by self?" He then went into a long philosophical disquisition about the seven diffcrent reasons why there is no self. There is nothing to hold on to and there's nothing in a way that we can name and designate in some effective way as being part of this transaction between ourselves and others.

Then he came to the end of this and he smiled, as he does. He has a wonderful smile. He said, "But, if there is no self, who is it who told you this?" One might well ask, who is it who told you all of this? He said a word in Tibetan that I remember very distinctly even though my Tibetan is not all that great. It was *Dag-tsam*. The translator translated it as "the mere eye." We might think that that had something to do with the eye, but what he was referring to was the mere self. I would translate that phrase actually not in the technical form of what sounds like a technical phrase, "mere eye." I would say, just me, just me, the Dalai Lama, or just me, you and me.

Buddhist philosophy, Buddhist wisdom, Buddhist views of no-self move back and forth between these two poles. The sharp analytical discrimination of the nature of the self that allows us to understand that there is nothing there that we can hold onto as a self, and then the wise and relaxed and calm experience of ourselves as active agents in the world of ordinary experience. That's the heart, it seems to me, of Buddhist philosophy and Buddhist wisdom.

Lecture Five
The Buddhist Community

Scope:

According to Buddhist tradition, the ascetics who heard the Buddha's first sermon became the first of many converts in the early Buddhist *Samgha*, or "community." During a long and productive teaching career, the Buddha attracted many disciples and laid the foundation for Buddhist monasticism, including orders of monks and nuns, as well as a sophisticated tradition of lay devotion and support. After the Buddha's death, attention shifted from the Buddha himself to the teachings and moral principles embodied in his *Dharma*. Monks recited his teaching and established a tradition of Buddhist scripture, while disputes in the early community anticipated the diversity and complexity of later Buddhist schools. Buddhist art and architecture shows us not only how Buddhists came to view the Buddha himself, but how they gave ritual and artistic expression to his teaching.

Outline

I. In the last three lectures, we have talked about the Buddha and the *Dharma*. It is now time to consider the third of the three refuges, the *Samgha*, or the community of the Buddha's disciples.

    A. As the Buddha wandered from town to town during his long teaching career, he gathered a large and diverse community of followers, including not just monks, such as Angulimala, but a community of nuns and lay supporters.

    B. The role of an ideal layperson is often represented by the figure of Anathapindika, the donor, or *danapati*, who purchased a pleasure grove for use by the Buddha and his community of monks. The word *danapati* means "lord of generosity."

        1. To understand the religious orientation of a typical Buddhist layperson, it is a good idea to start with this ideal.

        2. Generosity is not included as one of the five moral precepts, but for laypeople, generosity is a fundamental virtue.

3. Generosity makes it possible for monks and nuns to live the monastic life, and it gives laypeople an opportunity to live the ideal of renunciation in their own distinctive way.
4. As the monks go on their ritual morning begging round, the lay community provides them with food; this act of generosity ties laypeople into the act of "renunciation" that mirrors the more complete renunciation that will eventually lead to nirvana.
5. *Stupas* (reliquary mounds) became the prototype of places of worship—temples.
6. Buddhists often visit temples and make offerings at a shrine; they chant prayers and bow with their palms together.
7. The objective of worship is not merely to gain merit, but to help orient the Buddhist on the path to *nirvana.*

C. The Buddha created an order of nuns when he agreed to ordain Mahaprajapati Gautami, his great aunt.
  1. The Buddha insisted that nuns should abide by several additional restrictions and occupy a rank inferior to that of the monks.
  2. It was possible, however, for nuns to achieve awakening and nirvana, just like the monks.
  3. The community of nuns thrived in the early history of Buddhism and was important in the tradition's early expansion to other parts of Asia.
  4. Today, communities of nuns are found principally in China, Tibet, and Korea.

D. The monastic community began as a group of wanderers but soon evolved into a settled pattern of life, at least during a portion of the year.
  1. The rainy season, which arrives in northern India during the month of June or July, made the roads impassable and forced the monks to take refuge in residences, where they could be supported by a stable group of lay followers.
  2. At first, these were just temporary dwelling places, but they soon evolved into settled monasteries (*vihara*), where monks and nuns stayed not just for the rainy season, but for the entire year.

3. This pattern of monasticism, with its circle of lay supporters, has become the basic structure of Buddhist society and the bearer of Buddhist values.
4. The monasteries functioned as sophisticated centers of learning, as in Tibet.
5. But this form of social organization also made the Samgha vulnerable to persecution.

II. After the Buddha's death, the community confronted a significant problem of authority: To whom could the Buddha's disciples turn when they needed to resolve disputes about doctrine or discipline?

A. While the Buddha was alive, he suggested that they base their decisions on his own teaching.
1. This point was expressed in one of the Buddha's most famous teachings: "What point is there, Vakkali, in seeing this vile body? Whoever sees the Dharma sees me. Whoever sees me sees the Dharma."
2. The Buddha's stress on the teaching, rather than on his physical presence, was not problematic while he was still alive. If there were questions, people could always turn to the Buddha for help.
3. But when the Buddha was no longer present, the community had to find a way to fix the content of the Buddha's teaching so that it could function as a source of authority.

B. After the Buddha's parinirvana, senior monks convened a council to recite the Buddha's teaching and establish an authoritative body of doctrine and discipline.
1. Ananda recited the Buddha's doctrinal teachings. These became the *Sutta-pitaka*, or "basket of discourses."
2. Upali recited the Buddha's rules and regulations. These became the *Vinaya-pitaka*, or "basket of discipline."
3. Eventually, these were supplemented by a third basket, the *Abhidhamma*, which contained systematic reflection on the Buddha's teaching.

C. Together, these constitute the "three baskets" (*tripitaka*). It is common to call these three baskets a canon of Buddhist "scripture," although they were not written down for several centuries after the Buddha's death.

III. The contents of the Buddhist scriptures often are quite simple and pragmatic.

A. Discourses of the Buddha begin with a formula drawn from the oral tradition: "Thus have I heard. At one time the Buddha was dwelling at… and he said…."

B. These discourses are presented in a simple, down-to-earth style and offer a pragmatic approach to religious truth.

C. "The Discourse on Turning the Wheel of the Dharma" is considered the Buddha's first sermon, delivered after the Buddha had walked to Sarnath from the seat of his awakening and encountered a group of his old associates.

1. The text begins:

Thus have I heard. At one time the Lord was staying in the Deer Park at Isipatana near Banaras. There the Lord spoke to a group of five monks:

"O monks, someone who has gone forth into the monastic life should avoid two extremes. What are the two? One is devotion to passions and worldly pleasures. This is inferior, common, ordinary, unworthy, and unprofitable. The other is devotion to self-mortification. This is painful, unworthy, and unprofitable. By avoiding these two extremes, O monks, the Tathagata has realized the Middle Path. It gives vision, it gives knowledge, and it leads to calm, superior insight, awakening, and nirvana.

And what, O monks, is the Middle Path? It is the Noble Eightfold Path: right views, right thoughts, right speech, right action, right livelihood, right effort, right mindfulness, and right concentration. This, O monks, is the Middle Path realized by the Tathagata. It gives vision, it gives knowledge, and it leads to calm, superior insight, awakening, and nirvana."

From *Samyutta Nikaya* LVI.11, ed. M. Leon Feer (London: Pali Text Society, 1898), translated by Malcolm David Eckel.

2. After this account of the Middle Path, the Buddha goes on to give a brief account of the Four Noble Truths.

D. One of the simplest of the early sermons (and, in my view, one of the most significant) is the Fire Sermon.

    1. The Buddha begins by saying: "Bhikkhus, all is burning. And what is the all that is burning? Bhikkhus, the eye is burning, visible forms are burning, visual consciousness is burning.... Burning with what? Burning with the fire of lust, with the fire of hate, with the fire of delusion."

    2. The Buddha talks in the same way about the other senses.

E. The story of Malunkyaputta and the arrow is often cited as an example of the Buddha's concern for practical solutions to human problems rather than for fruitless doctrinal controversy.

    1. A man by the name of Malunkyaputta asked the Buddha to tell him whether the world was eternal, not eternal, finite, infinite; whether the soul was the same as the body; and whether the Buddha existed after death.

    2. The Buddha responded by comparing Malunkyaputta to a man who is shot by an arrow and will not let anyone remove it until he is told who shot it, what it was made of, and so on.

    3. The Buddha said that Malunkyaputta should be concerned with removing the arrow of suffering rather than with useless doctrinal speculations.

F. The Buddha's teaching is sometimes expressed in short, easily memorized verses, as in the collection known as the *Dhammapada*, or "The Words of the Teaching." These sayings are quite pithy and convey the simplicity of the Buddha's teaching. For example:

Not to do any evil, to cultivate good, to purify one's mind, this is the teaching of the Buddha.

You are your own protector. What other protector can there be? With yourself fully controlled, you obtain a protection that is hard to obtain.

There are a few people who cross to the other shore. The others merely run up and down the bank on this side.

From Rahula, *What the Buddha Taught* (New York: Grove Press, 1972), pp. 125–136.

IV. The second Buddhist council and the beginnings of Buddhist sectarianism.

  A. As the community expanded across northern India and monks adapted the teaching to new geographical and cultural situations, it became more difficult to enforce uniformity in doctrine or discipline.

  B. About a hundred years after the death of the Buddha, a dispute in the Samgha provoked a second Buddhist council.

  1. Historical accounts of this council are contradictory, and it is difficult to be certain about the source of the controversy or about its outcome.

  2. One account says that the council was provoked by the scandalous behavior of a monk named Mahadeva.

  3. Another says that it was provoked by disagreement over some of the prohibitions in traditional monastic discipline: one that prevented monks and nuns from using gold and silver and another that prevented them from carrying salt from one day to the next.

  C. Out of this dispute came a split between two major parties.

  1. The party known as the *Sthaviravada*, or "Doctrine of the Elders," was the predecessor of the *Theravada* tradition that now dominates the Buddhist countries of Southeast Asia (with the exception of Vietnam).

  2. The party known as the *Mahasamghika*, or "Great Community," was the predecessor of the *Mahayana* tradition that now dominates the Buddhist countries of North and East Asia.

  D. Later disputes took place over doctrine. For example, a group of Buddhists challenged the traditional understanding of the no-self doctrine by postulating the existence of a *pudgala*, or "person," that continued from one moment to the next. The pudgala was neither identical to the aggregates (which were momentary), nor was it different. Eventually, this doctrine was rejected by the majority of the community, but it remained influential in the Buddhist community for several centuries before it was finally refuted.

  E. Disputes in the Samgha eventually gave rise to 18 schools (*nikaya*), only one of which still survives in its traditional form: the *Theravada* (Pali for *Sthaviravada*) tradition of Southeast Asia.

Essential Reading:
Robinson and Johnson, *The Buddhist Religion*, ch. 3.

Supplementary Reading:
Strong, *The Experience of Buddhism*, ch. 3.

Questions to Consider:
1. What are the distinctive features of Buddhist social organization?
2. What are the strengths and weaknesses of this social system?

Lecture Five—Transcript
The Buddhist Community

In the last three lectures, we've talked together about the Buddha and the Dharma. It's now time for us to consider the third of the three refuges in the Buddhist tradition, the refuge that's called the *Samgha*, or the community of the Buddha's Disciples. You'll remember from the very beginning of our discussion about this, that one of the basic acts of devotion, you might say, or expressions in faith in the Buddhist tradition, is this threefold refuge: the statement that you take refuge in the Buddha, you take refuge in the Dharma, and you take refuge in the Samgha.

The Samgha is a community that gathered together in a rather complex way during the course of the Buddha's own lifetime, then was elaborated and carried on the Buddhist tradition through many centuries from that time to the present day. As the Buddha wandered from town to town during his own long teaching career in that middle region of the Ganges Basin where his career largely was carried on, he gathered together a large and diverse community of followers, including not just monks like Angulimala, but a community of nuns and a community of lay supporters. Our job in this lecture is to talk about the practices and traditions that are associated with the different parts of the Buddhist community.

We can start, I think appropriately, with the image of an ideal layperson. Why not? That's the kind of role that most of us would find ourselves in if we walked today into the middle of a Buddhist society. Often the ideal of a layperson is represented for Buddhists by a particular figure named Anathapindika, who was a donor or a *danapati*. The word *danapati* means simply a lord of generosity. Anathapindika, according to tradition, was a particularly generous person. He purchased a pleasure grove on the outskirts of a town for the use of the Buddha and his community of monks. According to the tradition, it cost him a lot of money to be able to provide this particular space for the use of the community.

To understand the religious orientation of a particular Buddhist layperson, it's a good idea for us to start with this ideal, the ideal of Anathapindika. Generosity is not included in the five moral precepts that we've already discussed, but for laypeople I think you'd probably have to say, in most Buddhist cultures, generosity is really the fundamental virtue. It's really the fundamental way that a layperson expresses a commitment to the maintenance of the monastic organization and to the pursuit of Buddhist values. Generosity makes it possible for monks and nuns to live the monastic life. It supports the monastery. It also gives laypeople an opportunity to live the ideal of renunciation that the monks and nuns are enacting, and to do it in their own distinctive way.

It might be useful for us to try to imagine, just so that we can place ourselves in some way within the context of a Buddhist community, simply to imagine what it would be like to be part of this transaction that goes on between monks and nuns on one side, and laypeople on the other, in which laypeople offer their support for the monastic community. Let's make a leap of the imagination and wake up some morning in a monastery in Thailand, or a monastery in Sri Lanka. It has to be early in the morning because the monks, you'll remember, haven't eaten since noon on the previous day. It is worth their while, I think, to get out on the road and begin to beg their food at an early hour.

We roll out of bed, and join the monks. They're in their saffron robes; their heads are shaved. They are living a very simple life and walking in a very focused and meditative way carrying their begging bowls, which are really the symbols of a Buddhist monastic vocation. The typical Buddhist word for a monk in Pali is *bhikkhu*. In Sanskrit it's *bhikshu*. It comes from a root that simply means to beg. Begging, in a sense, is the constitutive action that makes a person a Buddhist monk. We're joining the procession, the monks are walking very mindfully, almost as if they were engaging in a form of meditation, and they come across a town, a village, walk up to a house, stand in front of the house, and laypeople come out with food that they've cooked for the monks. The monks take the lid off their begging bowl and laypeople place food in each of the begging bowls. The monks then close the begging bowls and move on to another house until they've collected the food that they need, not just for themselves, but also for the monastery, for the other monks who are left back at the monastery, and go back and begin to eat the meal that will sustain them for the rest of the day.

This is a basic Buddhist action—very simple, but symbolically extremely rich. It's the action that really ties together, you might say, that sews together, the structure of a Buddhist community. Why would laypeople do this? Why would the lay supporters of the monastery provide food for the monks like this? Obviously, in order to support the monastery itself, but what benefit does it bring to them? If you asked Buddhist laypeople about this, they'll say that it has to do with the accumulation of merit, of good karma, good action, that will bring them a better rebirth in some future life. Also, I think, we would probably have to say, at least as outside observers, that it gives them a chance, in a distinctively layperson's style, to engage in an act of renunciation that mirrors the more complete and definitive renunciation that goes on in the monastic community itself. They're giving up themselves in the same way that the Buddha himself gave up all of his ties to the ordinary world in order to pursue the ideal of nirvana.

We're talking about Buddhism in this course in a comparative context. It's probably worth noting just in passing here that in many religious traditions, some that we're familiar with in our own environment, people are a little bit embarrassed to talk about the relationship between donations and the promoting of religion itself as if it were something that we shouldn't talk about, to talk about the relationship between money and the religious community. Here in the Buddhist tradition, this act of generosity that ties laypeople together with monks is one of the fundamental acts of devotion that is really the foundation of the community.

It probably is worth noting in passing that this act of generosity, while it is in many respects the foundation of a layperson's spiritual practice in Buddhism, is not the only thing that a layperson can do in order to acquire merit to ensure a better rebirth. There also is a tradition in Buddhism of worship in temple, at major pilgrimage sites, and also in Buddhist temples. This is an aspect of the Buddhist tradition that I mentioned, I think, very briefly when we were talking about the life story of the Buddha—when I said that at the death of the Buddha his body was cremated and his relics were distributed in a series of shrines known as *stupas*. These stupas really became the prototype for Buddhist centers of worship, and they have ramified and evolved now, not just into many different kinds of stupas—the architectural form of a stupa can be quite diverse across the Buddhist world—but also to temple structures as well, in which an image of the Buddha is located, or sometimes where some object that's associated in a particular way with the Buddha's life is enshrined.

Buddhists often, as part of their daily devotions, visit temples and make offerings in the shrine or offerings to the image. The kinds of offerings that they make are very similar to the kinds of offerings that are made in Hindu temples. They offer a lamp, a flower, some incense. It's very common—chants of prayer, chants in some devotional way, some expression of homage to the Buddha. Then, in that very basic gesture of respect that's found throughout the South Asian world, they put their palms together like this and bow gently to express homage to the Buddha, as well. These are the simple gestures of Buddhist worship, and you might say they provide the vocabulary for lay devotion in a Buddhist shrine.

The purpose of these gestures is not exactly to propitiate the Buddha. He's in parinirvana, or he has achieved parinirvana, and in a sense is not there to answer our prayers. It's a kind of meditation to acquire merit, to focus the mind, and to orient a person in some purposeful way on the path toward the pursuit of nirvana.

I mentioned earlier that the Buddhist community had not just monks, and of course not just laypeople, but also a tradition of nuns. We should spend a moment or two talking about how that tradition came to be, and what the role of nuns has been in Buddhist communities from the time of the Buddha to the present day.

The story about the formation of the order of nuns is strangely ambiguous, at least according to the traditions that have been passed on to us. The Buddha had a very ambivalent attitude toward the presence of women in the monastic order. The person who first pressed the point for him was a woman by the name of Mahaprajapati Gotami who played a very special role in the Buddha's life. She was the Buddha's aunt, and his foster mother who raised him when his mother died. She had indeed a special relationship with him. She was much impressed by the monastic organization and the monastic practice, and came to the Buddha and asked him if he would ordain her and a group of her friends to become nuns so that they could practice as the monks practiced. He told her that it was not appropriate to do that, and he sent her away. She came back several times more, and he sent her away again.

Finally, she was seen weeping outside the doors of a monastery, and a group of monks sent out the Buddha's trusty sidekick, the man who was really his principle attendant, whose name was Ananda, to ask what was wrong. She explained the situation to Ananda, and Ananda went to the Buddha and asked the Buddha if he would ordain Mahaprajapati and her friends in a separate order of nuns. He agreed to do it, but he imposed certain stipulations and certain special regulations on the order of nuns that seemed to have restricted their activities in a particular way. For example, he insisted that nuns would always occupy a rank inferior to that of the lowest monk. It was possible, however, for nuns to achieve awakening and to achieve nirvana just like the monks. The community of nuns that grew out of this very small initial community thrived in the early history of Buddhism and was important in the tradition's early expansion into other parts of Asia. Today, communities of nuns are found principally in China, Tibet, and Korea, although the order of nuns has died out in Southeast Asia.

You might ask whether this means that women have occupied subsidiary positions within the monastic organization throughout the tradition of Buddhism. I suppose we'd have to acknowledge that buried here in the origins of the order of nuns there is an image of the nuns' role in the community that seems to put it in a secondary place, but I would have to tell you from my own experience, I think experience counts when it comes to something like this, that the nuns that I've encountered in modern Buddhist communities have hardly been people who imagine themselves in a subservient or secondary position. Nuns today in the Korean tradition and in China and in Tibet occupy a very forceful, a very important, and very confident place within the larger system of practice within the Buddhist world. I think we'd have to say, to be fair, that, while the Buddha placed special restrictions on the tradition of practice of monasticism by women, he also opened up a great opportunity that has been enjoyed and taken advantage of by many strong and important women right through to the present day.

If we trace the history of the monastic community from the time of the Buddha on into subsequent generations, there are a few important transitions that we need to be aware of that have affected the shape of Buddhist monastic practice as we know it today. The monastic community began as a group of wanderers, but it soon evolved a settled pattern of life, at least during a portion of the year.

The rainy season, which arrives in northern India during the months of June or July, made the roads impassable and forced the monks to take refuge where they could be supported by a stable group of lay followers. At first, these were just temporary dwelling places, but soon they evolved into something that was fixed, stable, and allowed them to spend the entire year in a particular established setting. These settled monasteries are called *viharas*. They became eventually the central institution of Buddhist monasticism and the bearer of Buddhist values.

After the Buddha's death, the monks who lived in these monasteries, and also the monks who wandered in the traditional pattern of life across the landscape of northern India, faced a particularly important problem of authority. Who could the Buddha's disciples turn to when they needed to resolve disputes about doctrine or discipline? While he was alive, the Buddha suggested that they should base their decisions on the Buddha's own teaching. This point, as I mentioned in one of my earlier lectures, was expressed in one of the Buddha's most famous teachings. "What point is there," the Buddha said, "in seeing this vile physical body? Whoever sees the Dharma sees me, and whoever sees me sees the Dharma."

The Buddha's stress on his teaching, rather than on his physical presence, was obviously not going to be a very problematic thing for most people while the Buddha was actually alive. If there were any questions about what he meant or any points on which people needed to have something elaborated they could simply turn to the Buddha and say, "Oh, blessed one, help unravel for us the problem that we perceive in that discourse that you gave last week. It seemed on the face of it to be so puzzling." When the Buddha was no longer around, the community had to find a way to fix and settle the content of the Buddha's teaching so that it could function as a source of authority since there was no one else to whom the community could pass on the authority of the Buddha.

After the Buddha's parinirvana, a group of senior monks convened a counsel to recite the Buddha's teaching and establish an authoritative body of doctrine and disciplines, which was crucial actually, the formation of this early community. Even though they were working in an oral tradition where the teachings of the Buddha had been passed on by memorization from one person to another, their intention was to gather together an authoritative body of teaching that could then be passed on and serve as a source of authority for this early community.

They called on two people to recite what they had heard from the mouth of the Buddha himself. The first of these was Ananda, the attendant who had always helped the Buddha and followed him around on his teaching rounds. Ananda recited the Buddha's doctrinal teachings. These became the *Sutta-pitaka*, or the "basket of discourses," a collection of the doctrinal discourses of the Buddha. A man by the name of Upali recited the Buddha's rules and regulations. These became what was called the *Vinaya-pitaka*, or the "basket of discipline." Eventually these were supplemented by a third basket, the *Abhidhamma*, which contained a body of systematic reflection about the Buddha's teaching.

Together these "three baskets," the *tripitaka* constituted the canon of Buddhist scripture, although they were not very likely written down for several centuries after the death of the Buddha. The contents of Buddhist scripture often are quite simple and pragmatic. They clearly grow out of this oral transaction, this oral teaching that took place between the Buddha and his early disciples. The discourses of the Buddha begin with an oral formula. Almost always it comes very repetitively at the beginning of each of these *Suttas*, "Thus have I heard. At one time the Buddha was dwelling at such and such a place and he said the following."

We can get some sense of what this looks like in Buddhist tradition just by listening to the first few lines of probably the most famous of the Buddha's discourses, the discourse on the turning of the wheel of the law, or the turning of the wheel of Dharma. This is the first sermon. It was delivered after the Buddha had walked to Sarnath from the seat of his awakening and had encountered a group of his old associates. The Sutta starts like this: "Thus have I heard at one time the Lord was staying in the Deer Park at Isipatana near Banaras, and the Lord spoke to a group of five monks. 'Oh, monks, someone who has gone forth into the monastic life should avoid two extremes. What are these two? One is devotion to passions and worldly pleasures. That is inferior, common, unworthy, and unprofitable. The other is devotion to self-mortification. This is painful, unworthy, and unprofitable. By avoiding these two extremes, oh monks, the Tathagata," or the Buddha, "has realized the Middle Path. It gives vision, it gives knowledge and it leads to calm, to superior insight, to awakening, and to nirvana.'" He goes on from here to give a discussion of the Middle Path, to say more about what the practice of the Middle Path would be, and also to speak about the four noble truths that we discussed extensively in the last two lectures.

What would be some of the other typical examples of the Buddha's discourse? I'll just quote a few of them to you to give you an impression of the kinds of things that you're likely to encounter if you can dip a bit into the contents of the Buddhist canon. One of the simplest of the early sermons, and one of the sermons that I think is the most effective, is a sermon called the fire sermon. The Buddha begins by saying, "Oh, bhikkhus," oh, monks. "Everything is burning. And what do I mean when I say that everything is burning? Bhikkhus, the eye is burning, visible forms are burning. Visual consciousness is burning. Burning with what? Burning with the fire of lust, with the fire of hate, and with the fire of delusion." He then goes on from this initial comment to talk about all of the other senses as well.

Why, you might ask, is this so significant? It seems to be very simple, and in some respects really very obvious. What is it that makes this such an important sermon in the Buddhist tradition? I'd say in part because it establishes one of the very basic Buddhist metaphors, not just for the practice of ordinary meditation, but also for Buddhist theory about the nature of the self. We know that when you sit down in meditation, what you're trying to do is allow the mind to become calm, and allow many of its serious and intense attachments and aversions to things in this world to cool down and become quiet. This simple metaphor in some ways gives a roadmap for the practice of Buddhist meditation.

Practice is meant to cool the fires of distraction in this world. It also images for ourselves the nature of reality itself. It tells us that reality is constantly in a process of change, constantly burning as we add new things to it, and changing as those things are consumed and pass away.

There's another story that is commonly used to illustrate the practical orientation of the Buddha's teaching. It's well worth paying attention to, to get some sense of what the Buddha was like as a teacher. This is a story about a man named Malunkyaputta who came to the Buddha and told him, "I think you're an interesting teacher and somebody I might like to pay some attention to, but I'm not going to listen to anything that you say unless you can give me an answer to some basic questions. First of all, tell me, is the world eternal, or is it not eternal? Is it going to last forever, or is it going to pass away? Is it finite, or is it infinite? Is the soul the same as the body, or is it different? Does the Buddha exist after his death, or not?" These were Malunkyaputta questions.

The Buddha said to Malunkyaputta, "Listen. You remind me of a guy who was shot by a poisoned arrow and when people come running up to try to pull the arrow out, he says to them, 'Wait a minute. Don't pull that arrow out until you can tell me who it was who shot it, what the feathers are made of that sit at the end of the shaft, what the poison is that was stuck on the end of the arrow. Don't pull it out until you can answer all these questions.'" The Buddha said to Malunkyaputta, "Listen. What I'm offering you is a chance to pull the arrow of suffering out of your body, out of your personality. Don't ask me a lot of irrelevant and impractical questions. Take my teaching and use it as an antidote to suffering, and focus on the way it will bring you to nirvana."

This is an important teaching in the Buddhist tradition. I think it keeps the tradition focused on issues that are practical and have to do with the experience of human liberation and the relief of human suffering. If you trace the history of the early community a step further, another hundred years, an event takes place that is important for us in our later study of the evolution of Indian Buddhism. This is a second Buddhist council that was called about a hundred years after the parinirvana of the Buddha. Historical accounts of this council are contradictory. It's difficult to be certain about the sources of the controversy or about its outcome.

One account tells us that it was provoked by the scandalous behavior of a monk by the name of Mahadeva. Another account says that it was provoked by a disagreement over some of the prohibitions in traditional monastic discipline. One of these prohibitions was one that prevented monks and nuns from carrying salt and other kinds of condiments from one day to the next. You remember that monks are not supposed to carry food from one day to the next. The question was whether salt was to be prohibited as well.

Out of this dispute over these early monastic regulations came a split between two important parties in the Buddhist community. One was known as the *Sthaviravada*, or the "Doctrine of the Elders," and became the predecessor of the so-called *Theravada* tradition that now dominates the Buddhist countries in Southeast Asia today. That is all the Buddhist countries in Southeast Asia with the exception of Vietnam. The other party was known as the *Mahasamghika*, or "Great Community." This community became the predecessor of the *Mahayana* tradition that now dominates the Buddhist countries of north Asia. These disputes eventually gave rise to 18 schools, only one of which still survives in its traditional form. That's the school of the Theravada.

The picture we get finally of the Buddhist community, the Samgha, about two or three hundred years after the death of the Buddha, is a community that's expanding—it's thriving, it's complex, institutionally, but it also is beginning to show signs of division. And these divisions will be the major topic of our discussion in the next lecture when we take up the tradition of the Mahayana.

Lecture Six
Mahayana Buddhism—The Bodhisattva Ideal

Scope:

Near the beginning of the Common Era, a movement appeared that called itself the *Mahayana*, or "Great Vehicle," to contrast itself to the *Hinayana*, or "Lesser Vehicle." The word *Hinayana* was used to refer to previous Buddhist traditions. Although Mahayana texts trace their origin to the Buddha himself, the actual origin of Mahayana remains a mystery. The fundamental teaching of the Mahayana, however, is clear. The Mahayana promotes the ideal of the *bodhisattva*, or "future Buddha," who does not attempt to achieve nirvana as an individual goal but vows to return again and again in the cycle of samsara to seek the welfare of other living beings. Practitioners of the Mahayana develop the contemplative virtue of wisdom, together with the active virtue of compassion.

Outline

I. The *Mahayana*, or "Great Vehicle," emerged as a reform movement in the Indian Buddhist community around the beginning of the Common Era.

    A. Eventually, the Mahayana spread to China, Tibet, Japan, Korea, and Vietnam.

    B. The name *Mahayana* comes from the literature of the movement itself.

        1. Mahayana texts refer to themselves as a "Great Vehicle," in contrast to the *Hinayana*, or "Lesser Vehicle," that preceded it. The Hinayana is associated with the teaching of the 18 nikayas.

        2. An important source of this contrast is "the parable of the burning house" in the Lotus Sutra, in which a father (who represents the Buddha) tries to lure his children out of a burning house by promising each of them a different cart (or "vehicle"). When the children escape the house, he offers them "one vehicle," the Mahayana.

II. Indian legends trace the origin of the Mahayana to a "second turning of the wheel of Dharma" on the Vulture Peak in Rajagriha during the life of the Buddha. In other words, Mahayana texts claim to be the teaching of the Buddha himself, delivered to a special assembly of *bodhisattvas* from which other Buddhist practitioners (the Disciples and Solitary Buddhas) were excluded.

   A. Mahayana tradition goes on to say that the Mahayana was concealed for several centuries until the world was ready to receive it, then the sutras of the Mahayana were brought forth and promulgated across India.

   B. Scholars are uncertain about the actual origin of the Mahayana.

   1. There are suggestions in later Mahayana tradition that practitioners fasted and meditated in order to receive visions and revelations from great Buddhas and bodhisattvas. Perhaps some of the early texts of the Mahayana also came about in this way, although this could not be true of the more elaborate literary sutras of the Mahayana.

   2. Some scholars have suggested that the Mahayana arose in circles of laypeople who were worshippers of particular stupas. This view has now been discredited. It seems clear that the Mahayana had a strong monastic component from the very beginning.

III. One of the Mahayana tradition's most important innovations is the "bodhisattva ideal."

   A. A *bodhisattva* is a "Buddha-to-be" or "future Buddha" who does not attempt to go straight to nirvana but returns to this world to help others along the path.

   1. The bodhisattva ideal includes laymen and laywomen, as well as monks and nuns.

   2. A bodhisattva cultivates two important virtues: the wisdom (*Sanskrit praj–a*) that leads to nirvana and the compassion (*karuna*) that serves the interests of other sentient beings.

   3. The bodhisattva path can be represented as a two-way street or as a circle leading toward nirvana, then returning to the world of samsara.

B. The bodhisattva ideal is contrasted to the *arhant* ideal, in which a man or woman attempts to achieve nirvana for him- or herself by leaving the world of samsara behind.

C. Some people say that a bodhisattva renounces nirvana in order to lead all other beings to nirvana.

    1. This is not strictly accurate. A bodhisattva aspires to achieve Buddha-hood for the sake of all other beings.

    2. Eventually, even bodhisattvas become Buddhas, when their aspirations have reached fruition and their practice of the path is complete.

D. The bodhisattvas described in Mahayana literature are often human beings like ourselves, engaged fully in the world.

    1. Vimalakirti was a wise layperson who pretended that he was ill in order to teach a lesson to the Buddha's monastic disciples.

    2. A queen named Shrimala taught an important lesson about the Buddha nature.

    3. The young student Sudhana visited 50 different teachers and finally found Samantabhadra, a bodhisattva who had a vision of the universe that was vastly more complex and complete than anything we find in the earlier literature of this tradition.

    4. Such worldly figures had a radical effect on the spread of Buddhism. The tradition was no longer seen as a philosophy based solely on a monastic ideal, but one that had direct appeal for laymen and laywomen.

E. In classical Mahayana literature, the most important conceptual expression of the bodhisattva path is the "mind of awakening," or *bodhicitta*.

    1. The "mind of awakening" is a combination of wisdom and compassion.

    2. It is expressed in the form of an aspiration: "May I achieve Buddha-hood for the sake of all other beings!"

    3. It also can be viewed as the nature of one's own mind.

F. Formal accounts of the bodhisattva path are divided into a series of stages.

    1. One account of the path divides it into six perfections (*paramita*): generosity, moral conduct, patience, courage, mental concentration, and wisdom.

2. Another account divides the path into 10 stages (*bhumi*), incorporating and expanding the list of six perfections.

G. The easiest way to visualize the image of a bodhisattva may be simply through the tradition of Buddhist art. Unlike Buddhas, bodhisattvas wear the ornamentation of a layperson, and they often seem to be in motion, as if they were getting up from a moment of meditative concentration and reaching out to engage you in conversation.

Essential Reading:

Robinson and Johnson, *The Buddhist Religion*, ch. 4.

Supplementary Reading:

Strong, *The Experience of Buddhism*, ch. 4.

Questions to Consider:

1. Theravada Buddhists sometimes say that the Mahayana is a fabrication and not the teaching of the Buddha. Mahayana Buddhists say that it is the Buddha's only true teaching. How different do you think the Mahayana is? Are there important continuities that tie the Mahayana together with earlier traditions?

2. Mahayana Buddhists sometimes say that important figures in other religious traditions are really bodhisattvas. Would it be helpful to think of Jesus or Krishna, for example, as great bodhisattvas?

Lecture Six—Transcript
Mahayana Buddhism—The Bodhisattva Ideal

In our last lecture, we talked about the historical development of the Buddhist community in India. The last topic that I discussed with you had to do with the beginnings of Buddhist sectarianism, the beginning of that process that led to various competing and divergent traditions within the larger community. These were known eventually as the 18 nikayas or the 18 sects, of which now only one traditional sect still survives. That's the Theravada sect of South Asia.

Out of this process of sectarian division within the community, eventually came another major variety of Buddhism. The variety of Buddhism that we refer to today as the *Mahayana* or "Great Vehicle." This emerged in a way that is rather mysterious to us as a reform movement in the Indian Buddhist community around the beginning of the Common Era. Eventually, the Mahayana spread north to China, Tibet, Japan, Korea, and Vietnam. Those countries are the places where we would look today to study living Mahayana Buddhism.

The name *Mahayana* comes from the literature of the movement itself. The term is used to refer to the Mahayana as a great vehicle. That's what the word *Mahayana* means: "*maha*"—great, "*yana*"—vehicle. In contrast to the so-called *Hinayana* or "Lesser Vehicle" that preceded it. The *Hinayana* is associated with the teachings of those earlier 18 nikayas.

An important source of the contrast between the Mahayana and the Hinayana is the so-called "parable of the burning house" that's found in one of the most influential and one of the most wonderful Mahayana texts, a text that we refer to simply as the Lotus Sutra although the longer title of the Lotus Sutra is the *Saddharmapundarika*, the lotus of the true Dharma.

In the Lotus Sutra there's a story about a father, who represents the Buddha, who is standing outside his house, and the house is on fire. He looks up at the house, and the children inside the house are looking out of the windows, playing, and are completely unaware of the fact that the house is about to burn down. He says to them, "Hey kids, the house is on fire. Everything is burning." It's almost as if he's simply quoting that old fire sermon that we spoke about in the last lecture. The house is on fire. Everything is burning. Come on out of the house. The kids continue to play and are simply oblivious to the message that the father is conveying to them.

He says to them. "Okay kids, I've got some surprises for you out here. I've got separate carts, separate vehicles that each of you can play with if you come out of the house. For you, I have a goat cart; for somebody else, I have some other kind of cart. Come on out and receive your toys so that you can continue to play." The kids all come running out of the house, and the father says to them, "Delighted that you've made it outside but, let me tell you, I don't have a whole bunch of different carts, I have just one cart. This magnificently adorned thing that now all of you can play on together."

That cart obviously stands for the Mahayana, the one vehicle of the Buddha's teaching that's identified with the vehicle of the Mahayana. This story of the burning house has functioned in Mahayana tradition in an important way. First of all, it shows for adherence of the Mahayana that while the Buddha may have delivered many different teachings, teachings that may in many respects be contradictory. There, in the end, is only one teaching that is of ultimate significance, and that's the teaching of the Mahayana. The burning house is a place where people go traditionally in Asia to look for the assertion, look for the claim, that in the end there is a single, highest teaching presented by the Buddha during his own lifetime.

The story also gives a good image of another important doctrine in the Mahayana. This is the doctrine of skillful means. In fact, this is really the point that the story itself draws most attention to if you take a look at the story in its original form. The text asks the question when the story is over, did the father lie to the children when he said that there were many different vehicles that they could enjoy if they came out of the house? The answer that the text gives to that question is that the father didn't lie, he was simply using skillful means, using a particularly skillful technique in order to get the children to escape the fire that was about to burn them up. This too was an image, a very important image really, of the nature of Buddhist teaching within the tradition of the Mahayana. It's possible for the Buddha to use just about any kind of skillful teaching device to try to get people to escape the fire of suffering that consumes ordinary experience.

Indian legends, legends associated with the origin of the Mahayana, trace the Mahayana to a "second turning of the wheel of the Dharma" that took place on the Vulture Peak in Rajagriha, a particular place in northern India during the lifetime of the Buddha. In other words, the Mahayana texts claim to be the teaching of the Buddha himself, delivered to a special assembly of *bodhisattvas* or "future Buddhas," from which other kinds of Buddhist practitioners who were known in the texts as Disciples or Solitary Buddhas have been excluded. The Mahayana tradition goes on to say that this teaching was concealed for several centuries until the world finally was ready to receive it. Then the sutras of the Mahayana were brought forth and promulgated across India.

Scholars, those of us who study this tradition today, are uncertain now about what the actual origin of the Mahayana was. There are some suggestions in the later tradition that practitioners perhaps were fasting and meditating in order to receive visions of the Buddha, and perhaps in these visions they received some kind of extraordinary teaching. This could be true only of a few of the Mahayana texts that have come down to us. Many of them are clearly elaborate literary creations and are not the kind of thing that could be revealed to somebody simply in a vision or in a dream.

Some scholars used to suggest that the Mahayana arose in circles of laypeople who were worshipers at particular stupas. This view now has been almost completely abandoned because it seems that the Mahayana had strong monastic associations right from the very beginning.

If the origins of the Mahayana are so obscure, what do we know about the Mahayana, about the teaching of the Mahayana that we can hold onto to define for us this new movement? One of the Mahayana tradition's most important innovation was the teaching of the bodhisattvas ideal. You remember from our discussion of the life story of the Buddha that a bodhisattva is a Buddha-to-be, perhaps, or a future Buddha, someone who does not attempt to go straight to nirvana but who returns to this world in order to help others along the path. This is really the key to the bodhisattvas' ideal: returning into this world in order to help others move along the path to nirvana.

The bodhisattvas' ideal includes laymen and laywomen as well as monks and nuns. A bodhisattva cultivates two important virtues. One is the virtue of wisdom, *praj-a* in Sanskrit. We discussed this as part of the Buddha's Middle Path earlier. The other virtue is compassion, *karuna*, which serves the interests of other sentient beings. You can represent the bodhisattvas' path spatially as if it were perhaps a two-way street, or—maybe even better—as a circle that leads initially toward nirvana because bodhisattvas, like other practitioners of the Buddhist path, are attempting to lead themselves and others out of the experience of samsara and into the experience of nirvana, but they come back into this world in a cycle that helps them re-engage other people and help others along the path that they themselves are beginning to tread.

The bodhisattva's ideal is contrasted in the Buddhist tradition to the so-called *arhant* ideal, in which a man or a woman attempts to achieve nirvana for himself or herself by leaving the world of samsara behind. Some people say that a bodhisattva renounces nirvana in order to lead other beings eventually to nirvana. This is not accurate in a strict sense. A bodhisattva actually aspires to achieve Buddha-hood, to become a Buddha, for the sake of all other beings. Eventually even bodhisattvas become Buddhas when their aspirations are fulfilled and their practice of the path is complete.

Bodhisattvas that are described in Mahayana literature often are depicted as human beings like ourselves. It's one of the aspects of the tradition actually that's most accessible to ordinary people like you or me who are enmeshed in the difficulties and challenges of the ordinary lay world. One of my favorite Mahayana characters is a bodhisattva by the name of Vimalakirti, who was depicted in a particular Mahayana text that was very popular in China as a wise layperson who was a master of all of the important disciplines of the monastic life and yet lived the life of a layperson with a family and with an occupation and complete involvement in all of the challenges and difficulties of ordinary lay society.

According to the story, he pretended that he was sick in order to challenge the Buddha and his companions—his bodhisattva companions—to come and visit him, to comfort him, and to receive his teaching. Initially, all of them, at least according to the beginning of the story, tried to beg off because Vimalakirti was known to be a particularly harsh teacher and somebody who challenged many of their monastic preoccupations and their sense that the monastic life was really the only way that one could go about practicing Buddhism in any appropriate sense. Eventually a group of bodhisattvas surrounded by other people went off to visit Vimalakirti and engaged in a really remarkable series of discussions that involved interplay, challenging, undermining, threatening, and reforming and revising many of the basic categories of Buddhist experience.

One of the stories in the text that I particularly like—that became important philosophically in the later tradition—is a story about what is called the Dharma door of non-duality. Somebody asks, "In what way can you enter into the Dharma or the teaching of non-duality?" Non-duality is a concept that's used in the Mahayana tradition to speak about the doctrine of no-self. You might translate into language that is already familiar to us, translate this question as, in what way may I begin to understand the teaching of no-self? A bodhisattva gives a standard doctrinal answer to this. Another bodhisattva picks up the thread and discusses it a bit more. Eventually, the discussion begins to focus more and more on different ways of negating certain concepts about the nature of ultimate reality. Finally, someone turns to Vimalakirti and says, "We've all done our best to try to explain how we can begin to understand the concept of no-self. What do you say, Vimalakirti, to help us understand this important idea?" Vimalakirti said nothing at all.

It was the famous episode of Vimalakirti's silence. It was treated in the text as the definitive account of the Dharma door of non-duality, the entrance into the teaching of the Mahayana understanding of no-self. Vimalakirti is depicted in this text as a layperson—a wise layperson, an accomplished one, but nevertheless a person involved completely in the world of ordinary lay experience, but who is able to penetrate by his wisdom, by his understanding, to a deeper level, the understanding of the Dharma better than the monks and others who have come to visit him in his home. This aspect of Vimalakirti's experience is one of the reasons why he was so important in China, because the Chinese, as we'll see in a later lecture, were somewhat suspicious initially of Indian emphasis on monastic life. They appreciated an image of a person who could achieve all of the important degrees of insight that were associated with the monastic practice and yet still remain within the context of the family and ordinary lay experience.

Other bodhisattvas who might be mentioned or important in Mahayana literature are, for example, a queen by the name of Shrimala who has a sutra devoted entirely to her teaching and who taught an important lesson about the nature of the Buddha that also had significant philosophical implications in East Asia. Bodhisattvas are not always adults. Sometimes young people can function as important bodhisattvas in Mahayana literature. One of the most significant—again in East Asia, but certainly one of the most interesting in a literary sense in the Indian tradition—is a young student by the name of Sudhana, who visited 50 different teachers and then finally found a teacher by the name of Samantabhadra, who was a bodhisattva who gave him—by an application of almost magical power—a vision of the entire universe contained within a small structure so that Sudhana could understand the inter-relatedness of all of reality. This was a very positive and very strong image of the cosmos in its distinctive Mahayana form.

Worldly figures like this had a radical effect on the spread of Buddhism. The tradition was no longer seen as a philosophy based strictly on monasticism, but now was able to appeal directly to laymen and laywomen and draw them into the central issues of the practice of the Buddhist path. In classical Mahayana literature, the most important conceptual expression of the bodhisattva's path is a concept known as the mind of awakening, or the *bodhicitta*. The mind of awakening is visualized, in a sense, as a two-part concept—as the union of wisdom and compassion—and often is expressed not only in Mahayana philosophical literature, but also in the devotional practice of the Mahayana in the form of an aspiration: May I achieve Buddha-hood for the sake of all other beings?

This has two parts. May I, as an incipient bodhisattva, reach the stage of the Buddha, become a Buddha myself, to be as wise as the Buddha was and embody that quality of wisdom in my own experience? But may I do it for the sake of all other beings so that it be present in its power, in its efficacy and its insight and its wisdom for others? This involves the union of wisdom and compassion. It can be understood, and often is—in the context of the Mahayana—as an expression of the innate nature of your own mind: attempting to reach for the goal of Buddha-hood that lies in some kind of incipient sense within each one of us, as you might say, the first stirrings of our own attempt to realize our own liberated possibilities.

Formal accounts of the bodhisattva's path are divided into a series of stages, so when you begin to dig deeply into the literature you find that the path is divided up into a series of different practical levels that people have to go through in order to embody the bodhisattva ideal. One account of the path divides it into six perfections or parameters: generosity, moral conduct, patience, courage, mental concentration, and wisdom. You can see that some of these virtues are at least virtues that we've encountered before—moral conduct, *sila*, is identical to those five moral precepts that we saw were important for laypeople in the basic traditional account of the Buddhist path.

You also can see here that generosity is a significant virtue. We haven't seen that named before as part of the Buddhist path earlier, but here it clearly is a central feature in the tradition of the Mahayana. Patience is something that I suspect we probably imagine was significant in one way or another for Buddhists, but doesn't figure in the traditional accounts of the path that we've seen earlier. Likewise, so is courage. We know that this is a tradition that would take a certain amount of courageous effort, but also has not been named as a virtue earlier. The concept of mental concentration is, I think, significant to pause over because it names not simply that meditative practice that we've already discussed in our previous accounts of Buddhist practice, but begins to take on a rather distinctive cast in the Mahayana tradition.

There's a particular text that the Dalai Lama often uses to speak about the bodhisattva practice that talks about mental concentration, not so much as a meditative practice—although that does from time to time come into his discussion of bodhisattva discipline—but as a certain way of attempting to establish meditatively your relationship with another person. He often talks about meditation as having to do with the exchange of self and other people in an imaginative sense—as a way of transmuting hostile, aggressive, and negative emotional tendencies in the mind and in the personality into something that will eventually lead to Buddha-hood. He would say that if you feel envy toward somebody, or if you feel hatred toward somebody, or if there's something about another person that seems particularly offensive to you, the best way to try to deal with that feeling is not so much to try to suppress it, to try to make it go away, because then it will simply manifest itself again in another form, but to exchange yourself with the other person, to put yourself in the other person's shoes and feel that sense of envy, hatred, or resentment or whatever it may be toward yourself—and in that way begin to build, construct an antidote for yourself to the negative emotional states that seemed to be standing in the way of your practice of the bodhisattva path.

Another important practice that the Dalai Lama often speaks about that's not found in the same text, but also is significant in Tibetan meditation about bodhisattva discipline is the imaginative action of seeing all other people in the universe as being your mother from some previous life. In the Buddhist tradition, I don't suppose at this point we really need to remind ourselves that this is the case any longer. Samsara, the process of death and rebirth is going on, has been going on for so many lifetimes that everyone has been our mother probably and our father and our brother and our sister in one lifetime or another. What better way to imagine a sense of affection, concern for some other person than to begin to visualize the kind of relationship that they had with you in a previous life and the kind of care that they very well may have given you?

All of these are styles of meditation that go rather far beyond what we've talked about before, the simple concentration on the breath that is the basis of Buddhist meditation. They help take the meditative process a step forward in the direction of bodhisattva discipline and the development of compassion.

Another account of the bodhisattva path divides the path into 10 stages, incorporating these six perfections and then expanding them by adding some other important virtues as well, including the virtue of power and the virtue of skillful means. Skillful means that were spoken of in the context of the story about the father's teaching to the children in the parable of the burning house. What's important about these 10 stages is that, while the first six correspond in one way or another to the kinds of experiences that we might very well have in this world as ordinary human beings limited by the misconceptions or illusions that bind us in the world of samsara, once you get beyond the sixth stage—once you get beyond the stage of wisdom, when you begin to understand in a profound way the elusiveness and the illusory quality of ordinary life—it's possible to begin to develop extraordinary power so that you can begin to manipulate the process of samsara in some way that would respond to the needs of others in a profoundly powerful way.

It's hard to imagine what this might be, but let me give you an example of the kind of thing that I'm talking about. We were talking last time about the Buddhist practice of worship and how it's important for a layperson in the flow of ordinary experience occasionally to visit a temple, not just to give donations to monks to support the monastery, but to go and express a sense of worship to the Buddha, a sense of devotion and a sense of concern in such a way that will accrue merit and help provide a better rebirth in some future life. All of that is part of basic Buddhist practice. It's been built in to the practice of the Buddhist tradition from a very early time. In the Mahayana tradition, that practice of worship seems to expand itself almost in an exponential way.

We could do it as a simple experiment ourselves, I suspect, if we wanted to do that. Imagine that in front of us sits a golden Buddha. Let's create the Buddha for ourselves in our own minds as if he were sitting right here in space in front of us. Out of the body of this golden Buddha comes infinite numbers of rays, and at the end of each of these rays sits a whole array of other golden Buddhas so that we've created in front of ourselves—imaginatively—an array of Buddha images filling the space of this room and filling the space of the cosmos. Then we ourselves begin to make offerings to the Buddha, not just the flowers or the incense that we have readily at hand, but let's imagine that we go to the flower market, wherever that may be, the local flower market, and we gather up in our arms, perhaps in thousands of arms all the flowers that are available to us, not just in the flower market but in the entire universe, and we transport them to this room and offer them to these great imaginary golden Buddhas. How much merit accrues to us from that kind of a gesture?

In the Mahayana, that's a way—imaginatively—of expanding our ability to interact with the Buddha, and to build merit, and to acquire all of those powers and skills that will make ourselves effective bodhisattvas for other people in almost an exponential way. To simply expand our abilities into a sense—a feeling of power—that makes ourselves more than human, as if we were beginning to step into the realm of something divine. That's the kind of transition that takes place as you begin to move into the later stages of the bodhisattva path and begin to pass, as it were, beyond wisdom into something that looks a little bit more like the power of an extraordinary bodhisattva. Those powers are the beginning of the tradition of the devotional tradition of the Mahayana and the beginning of the concept of celestial Buddhas and bodhisattvas that will be the topic of our next lecture.

Lecture Seven
Celestial Buddhas and Bodhisattvas

Scope:

Along with the human beings who aspired to the *bodhisattva* ideal came an array of heavenly beings called "celestial" Buddhas and bodhisattvas. These celestial beings had accumulated the wisdom and compassion to save those who turned to them for help. Among the many important celestial bodhisattvas is Avalokiteshvara, the "Lord Who Looks Down" with compassion. In China, Avalokiteshvara is worshipped as the compassionate deity Kuan-yin. In Tibet, Avalokiteshvara's compassion is seen in the figure of the Dalai Lama. The most well known celestial Buddha is Amitabha, the "Buddha of Infinite Light." According to tradition, Amitabha resides in a celestial paradise known as the Pure Land and has vowed to save anyone who chants his name with faith. Devotion to Amitabha has had great influence in China and now is one of the most popular forms of Buddhism in Japan.

Outline

I. Advanced practitioners of the bodhisattva path (in the ninth or tenth stages) achieve extraordinary, superhuman powers.

    A. These powers make it possible for them to reside in the heavens (hence the name "celestial") and to function as the Buddhist equivalents of Hindu gods.

    B. Buddhists insist, however, that the great bodhisattvas have gone far beyond Hindu gods in their power and in their understanding of reality.

    C. Celestial bodhisattvas and Buddhas are the focus of devotion throughout the Mahayana world.

II. One of the most important celestial bodhisattvas in India and elsewhere in the Mahayana world is Avalokiteshvara, the "Lord Who Looks Down."

    A. Avalokiteshvara is considered to be the great bodhisattva of compassion.

        1. In the Lotus Sutra, Avalokiteshvara is described as a protean deity who takes any form that is appropriate to save the person who calls his name.

2. Devotees of Avalokiteshvara invoke his compassion by chanting the mantra *om manipadme hum.*

3. This mantra is sometimes translated, "Ah, the jewel in the lotus," in which *om* is the sacred syllable of the *Vedas* and *hum* is a sound that conveys power. As a mantra, however, the power of this phrase resides in the syllables themselves rather than in their meaning.

4. In India and Tibet, Avalokiteshvara was associated with Tara ("the Protectress"), who is the female manifestation of his compassion.

B. In Tibet, under the name Chenrezig, Avalokiteshvara is considered the patron deity of the Tibetan nation, taking form as the monkey who was the progenitor of the Tibetan people. He is also manifested in the succession of Dalai Lamas.

C. In China, Avalokiteshvara is known as Kuan-yin ("one who hears sounds"). During the T'ang Dynasty (618–907), Kuan-yin came to be pictured as a white-robed female deity who was particularly associated with the power to grant children.

III. Maitreya is venerated widely throughout the Buddhist world (including Theravada countries) as the Buddha of the future.

A. Maitreya is thought to reside in a Buddhist heaven known as *Tushita* ("Pleasurable").

B. Devotees of Maitreya not only invoke his aid, but—in some traditions—make a meditative ascent to Maitreya's heaven to see him face-to-face.

C. Hsuan-tsang, a well-known Chinese pilgrim who visited India in the seventh century, is said to have visualized Maitreya in heaven when he was captured and nearly sacrificed by pirates on a remote stretch of the *Ganges River.*

D. A popular and well-known image of Maitreya is Hotei, the fat, laughing Buddha of Chinese tradition.

IV. Ma–jushri ("charming splendor") is the bodhisattva of wisdom and the patron deity of scholars.

A. In his left hand, he carries a copy of the Mahayana sutra called the Perfection of Wisdom.

B. Ma–jushri is the Buddhist counterpart of the popular Hindu goddess Sarasvati, whose festivals are celebrated by schoolchildren across India.

V. The Buddha Amitabha ("Infinite Light") is a particularly influential example of a celestial Buddha. While still a bodhisattva, Amitabha vowed that when he became a Buddha, he would create a Pure Land known as *Sukhavati* ("Pleasurable").

A. Amitabha's vow stipulated that anyone who recollected his name, especially at the moment of death, would be reborn in this land.

1. A concise version of this story of salvation is found in a text known as the shorter Sukhavativyuha Sutra:

Then the Blessed One said to Shariputra: "In the west, Shariputra, many hundreds of thousands of Buddha-fields from here, there is a Buddha-field called the Land of Bliss. A perfectly awakened Buddha, by the name of Infinite Life [Amitayus], dwells in that land and preaches the Dharma. Why do you think it is called the Land of Bliss? In the Land of Bliss no living beings suffer any pain in body or mind, and they have immeasurable reasons for pleasure...

When any sons or daughters of good family hear the name of the Blessed Tathagata (Buddha) of Infinite Life and keep it in mind without distraction for one, two, three, four, five, six, or seven nights, then, at the moment of death, the Buddha of Infinite Life will stand before them, leading a group of bodhisattvas and surrounded by a crowd of disciples, and those sons or daughters of good family will die with minds secure. After their death, they will be born in the Land of Bliss, the Buddha-field of the Tathagata of Infinite Life.

This is what I have in mind, Shariputra, when I say that sons or daughters of good family should respectfully aspire for that Buddha-field.

From the shorter Sukhavativyuha Sutra, translated by Malcolm David Eckel.

2. The "recollection" of Amitabha is often expressed in the words *namo 'mitabhaya buddhaya* ("homage to Amitabha Buddha").

3. Like the invocation of Avalokiteshvara's name, this practice was a deliberate attempt to open the possibility of salvation to anyone who approached the deity with sincere faith.

B. Devotion to Amitabha Buddha (often known as Pure Land Buddhism) has been particularly influential in China and Japan.

1. The Pure Land tradition represents the largest Buddhist group in Japan today.

2. It is represented in North America by the Buddhist Churches of America.

C. The practice of Pure Land Buddhism raises a significant question about "salvation by faith."

1. How can a tradition that placed so much emphasis on self-reliance be transformed into a tradition of reliance on a celestial or otherworldly savior?

2. As surprising as it may seem, this tradition is a natural outgrowth of the Mahayana understanding of the bodhisattva's compassion. In the Mahayana, it is important not only to act with compassion but also to receive the compassion of others.

3. In the Mahayana, the passage to awakening has been stretched out over many lifetimes as a bodhisattva returns to this world again and again to help others.

4. The length of the bodhisattva path puts more emphasis on the virtues that help a person get started on the way to awakening. It is less important to have perfect wisdom, which can come later, than to develop the faith that begins the path.

5. It also is important to receive the compassion of others gratefully.

6. These changes of emphasis make possible a radically new view of salvation.

Essential Reading:

Robinson and Johnson, *The Buddhist Religion*, ch. 5.

Supplementary Reading:

Strong, *The Experience of Buddhism*, ch. 5.

Questions to Consider:

1. At the end of the last lecture, I asked a question about the continuity between the Mahayana and the Hinayana. That question becomes even more challenging when we consider Mahayana worship of celestial Buddhas and bodhisattvas. With this new information, how different do you think the Mahayana is from all that came before?

2. Are there still important continuities that tie the Mahayana and Hinayana together?

Lecture Seven—Transcript
Celestial Buddhas and Bodhisattvas

At the end of our last lecture, we did a little bit of an imaginative experiment in Mahayana Devotion. We created an image of a golden Buddha in front of us, and we multiplied the Buddha in what felt, to me anyway, as if it were an infinite number of times. Then we made an extravagantly large, imaginative act of devotion in front of this great, golden Buddha. The point of that, as you recall, was that in Mahayana Devotional tradition, the understanding of reality and the understanding of the Buddha's powers seem to expand almost infinitely. You have an image of the Buddha and an image of *bodhisattvas* acquiring, in an imaginative sense, powers that far surpass the powers we would ordinarily have as human beings in a religious context or in any kind of practical context in which we might normally live.

According to the doctrine of the Mahayana, the advanced practitioners of the bodhisattva path in the ninth or tenth stages, at the very end of the bodhisattva path, achieve extraordinary superhuman powers, like those powers that we were developing imaginatively for ourselves in the experiment that we just performed. These powers make it possible for bodhisattvas to reside in the heavens, not just in this world. Hence, they're given the name "*celestial bodhisattvas.*" These powers make it possible for them to function as the Buddhist equivalent of the Hindu gods. Buddhists insist, however, that the great bodhisattvas have gone far beyond the Hindu gods in their power and in the depth of their understanding of reality. Celestial bodhisattvas and Buddhas, like the ones that I've just described, are the focus of devotion throughout the Buddhist world. The topic for discussion in this lecture is the great pantheon of celestial bodhisattvas and Buddhas who provide the structure of devotion in the Mahayana world.

One of the most important celestial bodhisattvas in India and elsewhere in the Mahayana world is Avalokiteshvara, the "Lord Who Looks Down," presumably who looks down with compassion. Avalokiteshvara is considered to be the great bodhisattva of compassion, the great embodiment of that crucial Mahayana virtue. In the Lotus Sutra, Avalokiteshvara is described as a protean deity—that is a deity who can take many, many different forms in order to save anyone who recalls Avalokiteshvara or who calls on the name of Avalokiteshvara with some degree of conviction or faith.

Let me read a few lines from a devotional text to Avalokiteshvara that might give you some sense of how people visualized Avalokiteshvara in a devotional context: "Listen to the course of conduct of Avalokiteshvara. Listen and I will explain how, for unimaginable hundreds of eons, he purified himself by reaffirming his vows in the presence of thousands of millions of Buddhas. The systematic visual and auditory recollection of the bodhisattva Avalokiteshvara will, without fail, result in this world in the elimination of all the suffering and sorrows of living beings. If an evil-minded fiend intent on killing you throws you in a pit of coals, recall Avalokiteshvara, and the fire will be extinguished as though it were sprayed with water. If someone throws you into the depths of the ocean, the abode of sea serpents and monsters, recall Avalokiteshvara, the king of the waters, and you will never drown. He, Avalokiteshvara, has perfected all qualities. He looks down upon all beings with pity and kindness. Virtuous, a great ocean of virtue, he's worthy of praise. He has compassion for the world and will one day in the future become a Buddha. I bow down before him, Avalokiteshvara, who puts an end to all suffering and all fear."

This is a classic devotional statement about the significance of Avalokiteshvara in this Mahayana tradition. Avalokiteshvara can be invoked in lots of different ways in Buddhist practice. The text that I just read talks about recalling him, remembering his presence, and remembering his name. It's also possible to invoke Avalokiteshvara by using what's called a mantra, a sacred phrase that has power that can bring Avalokiteshvara's compassion to bear in any situation of danger. This is a mantra that Buddhists treat with extreme reverence.

Let me pass it on to you in case you encounter any danger any time soon in which you may need the help of Avalokiteshvara's compassion. The phrase goes like this: "*Om manipadme hum. Om manipadme hum.*" Some people have translated this as meaning, "Ah, the jewel in the lotus." That's a somewhat questionable translation in my view. What's most questionable is even the idea of translating it at all, because a mantra, typically in India, has power in the phrase itself. You don't need to know the meaning of it. All you have to do is recite those words, and they will bring to bear in any situation of danger the saving power of the bodhisattva Avalokiteshvara.

This is commonly used in Tibet. If you've seen pictures of a Tibetan mountain pass, or a Tibetan trail, or the wall of a Tibetan monastery, the mantra, *"Om manipadme hum"* is often carved on the wall of a monastery, or carved on stones and left in piles along the trail, or written on flags to fly off stone cairns on mountain passes, or written on the side of a prayer wheel that's spun in devotion to Avalokiteshvara. You could very well imagine that much of Tibetan devotional practice is a way of attempting to spin this mantra to fill the land of Tibet with the power of Avalokiteshvara's compassion.

In India and Tibet, and also in other corners of the Mahayana world, Avalokiteshvara is associated with a female bodhisattva by the name of Tara, a word that means simply, "the Protectress," someone who helps you cross over the flood of some sorrow to reach safety on the other side. She's the female manifestation of his compassion.

There's a wonderful devotional traditional associated also with her. It shows actually the importance in the Mahayana of the appearance of a tradition of figures who function like the goddesses of Hindu devotion. "Ohm, praise to the blessed noble, Tara. Your compassion truly extends equally to all beings on the pathways of rebirth. I am surely among those whom it embraces. Your unequalized capacity to safe beings shines like the sun on the dark passions, the impurities of the whole world, and I too, suffer and am tormented. Oh, the impure misdeeds that I have committed. Woe, woe, ill fated am I. I am blind even to the light of the sun. I am thirsty even on the banks of a refreshing icy mountain stream. I am poor even with access to abundant jewels in the minds of the Isle of Gems. And yet, it's possible for people to see in each of your hairs the expanse of heaven wherein dwell in bliss all of the Hindu gods, as well as humans, saints, and other divine beings, and all directions are pervaded by hundreds of Buddhas without end, which you have magically fashioned. Worthy of worship by the triple world, in your own being you contain all creatures. Some see you red like the sun, whose rays are redder than red lacquer or vermilion. Others see you blue like dust made of the pulverized fragments of precious sapphire. Some see you white, more dazzling than the ocean of milk and brighter than gold. Your form, like a crystal, takes on various aspects, changing according to the different things that are placed near it."

I read these to you in English, these little devotional texts. It would be nice to be able to chant them to you in Sanskrit so that you could place yourselves somehow within the auditory world of that Mahayana devotional tradition. You might very well imagine what this is like, to be sitting in a monastery, dusty place, dark very often, even in the daytime with a great image of Tara in front of us, candles lit in front of the image, and a group of monks and laypeople chanting the names of Tara and devotional phrases, and speaking about the way in which Tara's compassion fills the world with the possibility of salvation. This gives you a feeling, it's only a hint, I think, but it's just a feeling of the kind of devotional atmosphere that was created in the Mahayana tradition as people began to invoke, imagine, and make real in their own devotions these great celestial bodhisattvas like Avalokiteshvara and Tara.

Elsewhere in the Buddhist world, in Tibet, Avalokiteshvara is known by the name Chenrezig. Avalokiteshvara in Tibet is considered the patron deity of the Tibetan nation and takes form, according to Tibetan tradition, as the monkey who is the progenitor of the Tibetan race and who then eventually became manifested in the lineage of the Dalai Lamas. The Dalai Lama is considered a manifestation of Avalokiteshvara's compassion.

Often, I've had the experience of listening to the Dalai Lama lecture to American audiences. You know how there are certain standard questions that come up from time to time when a religious figure is presenting a new religious teaching in a certain setting. I've heard a number of different people ask the Dalai Lama what he thinks about the theory of evolution. They say, "It's a big issue here among some religious people in America about creation and the idea that human beings might have been descended from a monkey or an ape." The Dalai Lama always seems to laugh a little bit and he says, "In Tibet, we have this tradition that the Tibetan nation is actually descended from the union of a monkey and a goddess. We really don't have any problem with this theory of evolution." What he never says is that, "I, the Dalai Lama, was that monkey." We'll have to press him sometime and see if he would tell us a little bit about what it was like to set that tradition in motion.

In any case, Avalokiteshvara is understood as having a very special relationship with the Tibetan nation to protect and guide its destiny in this world. In China, Avalokiteshvara is known as Kuan-yin, a word that means, "one who hears sounds." That's a certain way of reading the Sanskrit name of Avalokiteshvara. During the T'ang Dynasty in China, which lasted from the year 618 to 907, Kuan-yin came to be pictured as a white-robed female deity who was particularly associated with the power to grant children. You often see, when you visit the shrines of Kuan-yin in China, particularly the great pilgrimage sites that are associated with Kuan-yin, you see pilgrims, predominantly women who travel to the shrines to pray for the welfare and prosperity of the family.

I visited a particularly important shrine to Kuan-yin on an island off the coast of southern China just a few years ago and had a chance, very happily, to interview some of the pilgrims who were there. I asked them why they came. This was almost always the answer that I received: That they had come, some from the Philippines, others from overseas Chinese communities, to pray for the benefit and welfare of their own families because Kuan-yin, as a celestial bodhisattva, is associated particularly with children and with the concerns of the family. Avalokiteshvara is a celestial bodhisattva who's had a lot of impact in the Buddhist world—not just in India, but in Tibet, China, and in other communities that have been affected by the Mahayana tradition.

Another important celestial bodhisattva is Maitreya, who even in the early tradition, was considered the future Buddha, the bodhisattva who was waiting in a heaven known as *Tushita* heaven until the time was right to descend into this world and set the teaching of Buddhism in motion once again. Devotees of Maitreya not only invoke his aid, but also in some traditions can make a visual ascent to Maitreya's heaven to see him face-to-face.

One of my favorite stories about Maitreya is a story that's told in the biography of a great Chinese pilgrim in India whose name was Hsuan-tsang, who visited India at the beginning of the seventh century of the Common Era. At one particular point in his journey, he was traveling down the Ganges River, entered a stretch of the river that was pretty desolate, and his convoy of travelers was attacked by a group of pirates who were devotees of the ferocious Hindu goddess, Durga, the Goddess of War. They captured the travelers, took them to the riverbanks, stripped them of all their possessions, and then decided that, because Hsuan-tsang was such an attractive and unusual looking person, they would make a sacrifice of

Hsuan-tsang to the goddess, Durga. They built a little altar on the side of the Ganges and prepared to sacrifice him to the goddess.

Hsuan-tsang, according to the story said, "Good sirs, I understand what your intentions are. Please, if you would be so kind, give me a few moments to collect my thoughts before I make the passage into the next world." He sat down and, instead of putting his mind in a state of calm and quiet contemplation, he made a visual ascent to the heaven of Maitreya. He visited Maitreya in Maitreya's throne room. At that moment, according to the story, of course, as he gazed on the face of Maitreya, a great storm rose on the Ganges and churned the river up into waves and blew over the trees and the pirates' boats. The pirates then threw themselves down in fear and asked who this magnificent and powerful Chinese monk was that they had attempted to sacrifice to the goddess. His identity was revealed, and they begged him to accept their repentance and to initiate them as Buddhist laypeople.

How much of this you want to believe is up to you. What's interesting to me is that it depicts for us in the story told during the T'ang Dynasty in China, a particular image of devotion to Maitreya, an image in which Maitreya can be visualized in some heavenly realm and in such a way that his aid and his power will be made present in this world.

Other ways to encounter Maitreya would be fairly accessible to most of us, would be in that very well known image of Maitreya as Hotei,—the fat, laughing Buddha of the Chinese tradition. If you've ever looked at these little images of the laughing Buddha, which are pretty widely available in our world, you'll notice that he often carries a big bag. That bag has gifts that are meant to satisfy the needs of all sentient beings. Maitreya is another important way of imaging the power of the celestial bodhisattvas.

Another bodhisattva who's worth knowing about is Ma-jushri, whose name means "charming splendor." Ma-jushri is the bodhisattva of wisdom and the patron deity of scholars. In his left hand, he carries a copy of the Mahayana sutras that are known as the Perfection of Wisdom, which functions as the basis of the scholastic tradition of the Mahayana. He's the Buddhist counterpart of the popular Hindu goddess, Sarasvati, whose festivals are commonly celebrated by schoolchildren across India. I found when I work with Tibetan monks on philosophical texts, that monks often are very acutely conscious of the presence of Ma-jushri as a force of inspiration for scholars.

I was reading a particularly difficult text one time with a Tibetan monk in a monastery in New Jersey. We worked and worked and worked very intensively for about a week. As we began to get near the end of the text, it began to be a little clearer to us what was going on. We were able to read the text more easily and make faster progress through some of its difficult sections. Finally, we came to the end of it and we closed it, he looked at me and smiled and said, "Ma-jushri has smiled upon us today." I must say in some uncanny way I felt that the presence of Ma-jushri had graced us at that moment, that we had been given a quality of wisdom and insight that helped us make our way through that difficult forest of philosophical vocabulary. In any case, Ma-jushri has been an important bodhisattva in the Mahayana tradition in India, Tibet, China, and elsewhere where the Mahayana is popularly practiced.

Celestial bodhisattvas are obviously important in the tradition, but it's important for us to be aware also that these celestial deities come in another form as well, in the form of celestial Buddhas. The devotional tradition of the Mahayana is directed not just at bodhisattva figures, but at figures who have completed the path and who have entered the stage of Buddha-hood as well. One of the most important of these, one of the ones that you're most likely to encounter in the contemporary world, is the celestial Buddha Amitabha, whose name means "Infinite Light." The story about Amitabha is that he once took a vow that when he became a Buddha, he would create a Pure Land known as *Sukhavati*, which means simply, "the pleasurable land." When anyone chanted his name or recollected his presence, especially at the moment of death, they would be reborn in this land.

Let me just read you a concise version of this story of salvation that's associated with the celestial Buddha Amitabha. It comes from a text known as the Shorter Sukhavativyuha Sutra. "Then the blessed one said to Shariputra, 'In the West, Shariputra, many hundreds of thousands of Buddha fields from here, there is a Buddha field called the Land of Bliss. A perfectly awakened Buddha by the name of Infinite Life (the name is Amitayus, which is an alternate name for Amitabha Buddha) dwells in that land and preaches the Dharma. Why do you think it is called the Land of Bliss? In the Land of Bliss no living beings suffer any pain in body or mind, and they have immeasurable reasons for pleasure. When any sons or daughters of good family hear the name of the blessed Buddha of Infinite Life, and keep it in mind without distraction for one or more or seven nights, then, at the moment of death, the Buddha of Infinite Light will stand before them, leading a group of bodhisattvas and surrounded by a crowd of disciples, and those sons or daughters of good family will die with minds secure. After their death, they will be born in the Land of Bliss, the Buddha-field of the Tathagata of Infinite Light.'"

The "recollection" of Amitabha, the way you bring Amitabha to mind in order to make his compassion active in your experience according to this tradition, is often expressed in the words, *namo 'mitabhaya buddhaya* which means simply "homage to Amitabha Buddha." The word, *namo*, at the beginning of this phrase is the same word that you use to name the gesture that's very commonly used to greet people in India. You put your palms together and say, in contemporary India, "*Namaste.*" Namas is this word namo. While we translate it as homage to Amitabha Buddha, it simply is a form of greeting, simply to greet Amitabha by name. Like the invocation of Avalokiteshvara that we talked about a few minutes ago, this practice is a deliberate attempt to open up the possibility of salvation to anyone who approaches the deity with some kind of sincere faith.

If you're taking this course in the context of the great religious traditions of the world, you might well want to ask yourselves whether we have here, in this practice of invoking the name of Amitabha Buddha, an example of the kind of name theology that often pops up in other religious traditions around the world. It's very common in Hinduism, for example, to invoke the presence of a deity by chanting the name of the deity. It's true also in Islam and in some forms of Christian devotion, as well. Why do people do that? It seems so simple. It seems too obvious. Why would that be such a fundamental practice in the religious traditions of the world?

I think sometimes that it comes out of an impulse that lots of different religious traditions share, that, while religion can become extremely complicated, as of course it is, and I'm sure much of what we've talked about in our discussion of Buddhism here seems immensely more complicated than religious practice needs to be much of the time, at the core of many traditions of religious devotion lies a simple calling upon the name of the deity, as if to say in the midst of all of the complexity that we experience in religious life, what we really are required to do is simply name the deity and place ourselves, in some kind of grateful and open-hearted way, in the hands of the deity and welcome the deity's salvation. I've often found in my own travels that experiences like this take me into the heart of the tradition more directly than many of the more complicated forms of study that I engage in.

I was sitting once with my daughter, actually, on the deck of a beautiful hotel in India at dusk as the parrots were flying around us and the sun was setting into the haze over the hills at the edge of the lake. In the quiet of the early evening, we could hear a chant coming across the lake that said simply, "*Jay Ram, Jay Ram.*" What does it mean? "Oh, God. Oh, God. Oh, God." A simple invocation of the deity like the invocation of Amitabha that we're speaking about here, to bring the deity's compassion and make it present in your own experience.

Devotion to Amitabha Buddha in the form that we've just been talking about is often known as Pure Land Buddhism. It's been particularly influential in China and Japan. Pure Land Buddhism represents the largest Buddhist group in Japan today. It's represented in North America by an organization that's called the Buddhist Churches of America. If you live on the West Coast, you might very well want to visit one of these churches and study the practice of this devotional tradition more directly. The practice of Pure Land Buddhism raises a significant historical question for us as students of this tradition. How could a religion like Buddhism that placed so much emphasis on self-reliance now be transformed into a tradition of reliance on the power of a celestial or other-worldly savior? A very interesting and important historical question.

As surprising as it may seem, this new form of Buddhist practice does not need to be understood as a foreign intrusion into the history of Buddhism. We can see it as a natural outgrowth of the Mahayana understanding of the bodhisattvas' compassion. In the Mahayana, it's important to act with compassion. We've talked about that, to be a bodhisattva. It also is important to receive the compassion of others. In the Mahayana, the passage to enlightenment, this path that the bodhisattva attempts to tread, has been stretched out over so many lifetimes, and the bodhisattva returns to this world again and again so many times, that the stress now lies not so much on the conclusion of the path, but on that quality of mind and heart that allows us to enter the path and begin to get access to the compassion of great bodhisattvas.

In this devotional tradition, simply to begin the path is already to begin to experience the fullness of all of the compassion that has been set in motion by Buddhism bodhisattvas in previous lives. That makes it possible, strangely enough, as odd as it might seem, for a tradition of self-reliance now to manifest itself in a tradition that puts immense stress on reliance on the compassion of others.

Lecture Eight
Emptiness

Scope:

At the heart of Mahayana tradition lies the paradoxical concept of Emptiness. Mahayana texts claim that nothing exists in its own right. In other words, they say that everything is "empty" of identity. Like the concept of nirvana, Emptiness seems at first to be extremely negative, but the Mahayana tradition claims that it is exactly the opposite. Mahayana texts insist that "everything is possible for someone for whom Emptiness is possible." The doctrine of Emptiness was elaborated in a sophisticated tradition of Mahayana philosophy and gave rise to a radically new way of viewing the Buddha. In Tantric Buddhism, also known as the *Vajrayana* ("Diamond Vehicle"), the Buddha can be visualized not just as the peaceful figure we know from earlier Buddhist art, but also as a wrathful deity and as the intimate union of male and female.

Outline

I. The Mahayana introduced many important changes in the Indian Buddhist tradition, but none was as profound or as far-reaching as the concept of Emptiness.

    A. Emptiness challenged and undermined many of the rigid categories of traditional Buddhism.

    B. But it also introduced a new spirit of affirmation and possibility.

    C. A balanced understanding of Emptiness has to account for both its positive and its negative dimensions.

II. Emptiness can be understood as an extension of the traditional Buddhist doctrine of no-self.

    A. In the Hindu tradition, particularly in the *Upanishads*, it was understood that each person has a permanent or eternal self (*atman*).

    B. The Theravada Buddhist tradition denies that there is any permanent self.

        1. According to the Theravada, the so-called "self" is made up of a series of momentary phenomena known as *dhammas* (Pali) or *dharmas* (Sanskrit).

2. These momentary phenomena give the illusion of continuity, like the moments of flowing water that make up the current of a river or the flickers of burning gas that make up the flame of a candle.

C. The Mahayana takes the concept of no-self a step further: It denies the reality of a permanent self and the reality of the momentary phenomena that make up the flow of the personality.
   1. This Mahayana position is expressed by saying that everything is "empty" (*shunya*) of identity (*svabhava* or *atman*).
   2. The nature of all things is simply their "Emptiness" (*shunyata*).

D. By rejecting the idea that the personality is made up of real moments, the Mahayana completely reorients the conceptual framework of Buddhism.

III. The concept of Emptiness has several important consequences, some of which are negative and some, extremely positive.

A. If everything is empty of real identity, there can be no real difference between any two things. As a result, Mahayana texts often equate Emptiness with "non-duality."
   1. If everything is empty, there can be no difference or "duality" between nirvana and samsara, and there can be no difference between ourselves and the Buddha.
   2. This means that nirvana is right here, at this moment, if we can only understand it. It also means that we are already Buddhas, if we understand that the nature of ourselves is no different from the Buddha.

B. According to the doctrine of Emptiness, the bodhisattva does not turn away from nirvana purely for altruistic reasons.
   1. In seeking nirvana, the bodhisattva finds that there is no nirvana apart from samsara.
   2. This means that nirvana can be attained only by returning to the context of samsara.

C. A correct understanding of Emptiness requires a balance between two different perspectives or "truths."
   1. Ultimately, all things are empty, and nothing is real.
   2. Conventionally, from the point of view of ordinary life, it is possible to take things seriously.

D. The doctrine of Emptiness was given sophisticated philosophical expression in the Indian monastic tradition, and it still is the intellectual focus of Tibetan monastic education.

IV. One of the most striking expressions of Emptiness appeared in the tradition known as Buddhist Tantra.

    A. Tantric Buddhism began to emerge in India during the sixth century of the Common Era.

        1. Tantra is known as the *Vajrayana* ("Diamond Vehicle") and as the *Mantrayana* ("Vehicle of Powerful Words").

        2. Tantric Buddhism shares many important concepts, symbols, and ritual practices with its Tantric counterparts in other Indian traditions.

    B. How is the Tantric tradition related to earlier forms of Buddhism?

        1. Sometimes, the Tantric tradition is described as a separate "vehicle" alongside the Hinayana and the Mahayana.

        2. But it is more helpful and more accurate to consider Tantra an extension of the values of the Mahayana.

V. Buddhist Tantra was based on a radical extension of the concept of non-duality.

    A. The Buddha was pictured not just as a serene and peaceful figure but one that is full of passion and wrath.

        1. These images are known as "wrathful Buddhas."

        2. Tantric texts say that poisonous emotions, such as passion and wrath, can be removed by cultivating and transmuting the emotions themselves.

Those who do not perceive the truth think in terms of samsara and nirvana, but those who perceive the truth think neither of samsara nor nirvana. Discriminating thought is then the great demon that produces the ocean of samsara. But being free of this discriminating thought, the great ones are freed from the bonds of existence....

Just as water that has entered the ear may be removed by water and just as a thorn may be removed by a thorn, so those who know remove passion by passion itself. Just as a washerman removes the grime from a garment by means of grime, so the wise man renders himself free of impurity by means of impurity itself.

From the Cittavisuddhiprakarana, translated by David Snellgrove, in Edward Conze, ed., *Buddhist Texts through the Ages* (New York: Harper and Row, 1964), p. 221.

B. In Tantric tradition, Buddhas can also be pictured as the union of male and female.
    1. These figures are known as *yab-yum* images, from a Tibetan word that means "male and female" or "father and mother."
    2. People often ask whether yab-yum images were meant to suggest that sexual union functions literally as a form of Buddha-hood. This question is difficult to answer because the texts are not easy to interpret. There is no question, in some situations, that a ritual of sexual union played a role in Tantric meditation. But it is more common for these images to function as symbolic representations of a mind that has transcended all dualities, including the distinction between the sexes.

C. Tantric ritual often arranges images of the Buddha in the form of a sacred circle, or *mandala.*
    1. A basic mandala contains the images of four Buddhas, located at each of the cardinal directions, with a fifth Buddha in the center to represent ultimate reality.
    2. In Tantric ritual, practitioners learn to unify their own personalities (as miniature mandalas) with the mandala of the five Buddhas and with the mandala of the universe as a whole.

D. Tantric tradition has had enormous impact on the culture of Tibet and has played a significant role in the development of Buddhism in China and Japan.

Essential Reading:

Robinson and Johnson, *The Buddhist Religion*, ch. 4, section 2; ch. 6.

Supplementary Reading:

Strong, *The Experience of Buddhism*, ch. 4, sections 2–3; ch. 5, section 5.

Eckel, *To See the Buddha*.

White, *Tantra in Practice*, Introduction and chs. 1, 14, 30.

Questions to Consider:

1. The doctrine of Emptiness sharpens many of our earlier questions about the negative characteristics of Buddhist thought. How does the idea that everything is "empty of individual identity" make a person feel more wise or more free?

2. When Western scholars first encountered Tantric Buddhism, they thought that it was a corruption of the Buddha's teaching, and they blamed it for the eventual destruction of Buddhism in India. Do you think Tantra distorts or corrupts the Buddha's teaching? Or would you be more inclined to think of it as a rediscovery or intensification of the basic insight in the Buddha's teaching?

Lecture Eight—Transcript
Emptiness

In the last two lectures, we've seen that the Mahayana tradition introduced a lot of important changes into the community and practice of Indian Buddhism. We talked about the bodhisattva ideal, and discussed some scriptural examples of classic bodhisattvas. We talked about celestial bodhisattvas and celestial Buddhas, and discussed at the end of our last lecture this great question of salvation by faith in the Mahayana. We talked for a bit about whether that was a tradition that we would recognize as being Buddhist in some fundamental sense, or whether it was an intrusion, some sort of borrowing from a religious tradition from the outside. These were all significant new elements in the Indian Buddhist community, and profoundly changed the experience of Buddhism in India.

They were not the only important changes that the Mahayana introduced. The Mahayana also developed a new concept of reality, a new way of approaching the old doctrine of no-self. We call this the doctrine of Emptiness. In this lecture, we're going to take a very close look at the significance of the doctrine of Emptiness, and allow it to lead us into the philosophical heart of the Mahayana.

The doctrine of Emptiness challenged and undermined a lot of the old rigid categories of traditional Buddhism. In that sense, it was quite negative. It involved a critique of the traditional structure of the Buddhist path. It also introduced a new and expansive spirit of affirmation and possibility. As we ponder this concept, as we try to get some sense of its contours and its shape, we need to be able to account for both its positive and its negative dimensions, as has been true in other aspects of the Buddhist tradition.

The best way for us to begin to understand the doctrine of Emptiness is to see it as an extension of the traditional Buddhist doctrine of no-self. In the Hindu tradition, particularly in the classic texts of the *Veda* that are known as the *Upanishads*, it was understood that each person had a permanent or eternal self. The Theravada Buddhist tradition distinguished itself from this old Hindu doctrine by denying that there was any permanent self at all. The word for "self" in this tradition is *atman*. The no-self-doctrine in Theravada is the doctrine of no atman. Or in Pali, *anatha*.

According to the Theravada, what we call the self is made up of a series of momentary phenomena that are known in this traditional system as "*dhammas*" in Pali, or "*dharmas*" in Sanskrit. This is the same word, of course, as the word Dharma that we use to refer to the Buddha's teaching. Here we spell it with a small lower case "d" and discuss it in the plural. These momentary phenomena give the illusion of some kind of continuity, like the moments of flowing water in a river, or the flickers of burning gas that make up the flame of a candle.

The Mahayana tradition took this concept of no-self a step further. It denied the reality of a permanent self that lingers from one moment to the next, just as the Theravada tradition did. It also denies the reality of these momentary phenomena that make up the flow of the personality. This is a crucial difference. This Mahayana position is expressed by saying that everything is empty—the word here is *shunya* in Sanskrit—empty of identity. The word for "identity" would be *svabhava* in Sanskrit, or simply *atman* the old word for "self." This means, in the technical terminology of the Mahayana, that all things are empty of self in their nature. The nature of all things is simply their Emptiness. Hence the name "Emptiness" as a reference for this doctrine.

By rejecting the idea that the personality is made up of real moments, the Mahayana completely reoriented the conceptual framework of Buddhism. The best way for us to explore it together is simply to ask ourselves what some of its most important implications might be.

First of these is the concept of non-duality. If everything is empty of real identity, then there can't be any real difference between any two things. As a result, Mahayana texts often equate the concept of Emptiness with the concept of "non-duality." What does this mean? If everything is empty, then there can't be any difference or any "duality" between nirvana and samsara. There can't be any difference between ourselves and the Buddha. This is a radical statement that the Mahayana tradition is making. This means that nirvana is right here at this moment, if we can only understand it correctly. There is no real barrier for us that would prevent us from experiencing nirvana right now in this moment.

It also means that we are already Buddhas, at least potentially, if we can understand the nature of ourselves as being no different from the nature of the Buddha. This is a crucial conceptual shift. You can see that it opens up all sorts of new possibilities for us in the study of this tradition. We looked, for example, just a couple of lectures ago, at this great experiment of imagining a golden Buddha in front of us to whom we offer imaginary flowers. I suppose, in the back of our minds at that moment, there was some question about how real this transaction was. Was the Buddha really there? Were our offerings real offerings to the Buddha?

In the context of Emptiness, we can see that the Mahayana tradition is telling us that this imaginary gesture, this visualization of the Buddha, to whom we offer imaginary flowers, is just as real as any Buddha would be. What's important is the imaginative process that takes us through that devotional action. The doctrine of Emptiness makes it possible for us to offer ourselves in that kind of setting in a way that's effective. In the pursuit of the bodhisattva path, it would not have been true in the earlier tradition. One of the important consequences of the concept of Emptiness is simply this idea of non-duality, an idea that denies the distinction between things, but also opens up an extraordinary array of new possibilities in meditation and in acts of devotion.

Another important consequence of the doctrine of non-duality has to do with the practice of the bodhisattva path. We said before that bodhisattvas turn away from nirvana in order to come back into this world to help others. This is altruistic, and I suppose it's entirely admirable that bodhisattvas are concerned enough about other people to help them along on the path. We can see now, with the doctrine of Emptiness, that the bodhisattva doesn't just do this for altruistic reasons, because there is no nirvana out there that's different from samsara that the bodhisattva can seek and then in a sense reside in, to the exclusion of the experience of others in samsara. If the bodhisattva is really seeking to become a Buddha, really seeking to become enlightened, the bodhisattva has to follow that path and experience that process in the world of samsara itself. The bodhisattva comes back into the Samsaric world, not just to help others, but really to pursue Buddha-hood for the bodhisattva's own sake. There's another important change that puts the basic teachings of the Mahayana in a slightly different perspective.

Another important consequence of Emptiness is really more philosophical in form. The Mahayana tradition developed a doctrine of two truths, or two different perspectives that can be used to view anything that is part of our ordinary experience. From the ultimate perspective, according to the Mahayana, all things are empty of any identity, so nothing is real. Everything that we experience is simply part of the flow of illusion that we have experienced from beginningless time. What we seem to see as real around us is not, in the end, ultimately, something that has any real identity.

This is not to say that our experience, the experience that we have together, the experience that we have of the reality that surrounds us, isn't real in a pragmatic or conventional sense. The Mahayana tradition insists that, whenever we approach any particular question or any particular reality in this world, we have to hold two perspectives together: An ultimate perspective in which we acknowledge that what seems so apparently real is nothing but an illusion, and a conventional perspective in which we take it seriously and respect its reality and begin to work with it in some kind of positive sense. This means that the bodhisattva, or, for that matter, a Mahayana philosopher, has to constantly hold these two perspectives together in approaching any particular question. They sometimes say that you have to hold them together as if you were holding a jewel in the palm of your hand, so that you can, at the same time, see the jewel and see through the jewel to see the palm, to see the hand that lies underneath it.

What does this mean in practice? This is a philosophical distinction, and I suspect most of you are wondering how this would actually work out in the life of a Mahayana Buddhist thinker. Probably the best example to go to in order to understand the impact of this idea is an example that I've already mentioned to you in a previous lecture, the example of the Dalai Lama's lecture about the doctrine of noself.

You may recall that the Dalai Lama when he was asked to give a presentation about the Buddhist idea of the self, started out by talking about compassion. When I first mentioned this to you, I don't think we knew how important an idea that was in the Mahayana. We now can see that he was beginning from a central Mahayana concept. If you want to know yourself, be compassionate to others. It's a pretty simple Mahayana injunction. Learn about yourself by giving of yourself to other people and making yourself available to them in a compassionate sense. That's a pretty good starting point. It's what you would call, I think, in Mahayana tradition, a conventional starting point. It's the starting point in which you assume, "I'm real. You're real. Let's see if there's something I can do to be of some benefit to you."

The Dalai Lama paused for a moment and he said, "When we talk about self in the Mahayana tradition, we can't just affirm that self in some sort of naïve and positive way. We have to scrutinize it carefully and ask whether the world self refers to anything in the end that is real." Then he began a long discourse about the nature of the self, in which he gave a whole series of reasons in philosophical Tibetan why there can't be any identity in anything, not only in the stream of phenomena that appears to continue from one moment to the next, but in the individual moments of experience. He came to a point that in some ways seemed quite negative and almost bewildering, in which he had denied the reality of everything. He paused a second time. He stopped and said, "If there is no identity and no reality in anything, then who is it who has said this to you? Who gave you this teaching?" He smiled gently and used the Tibetan phrase, "*Dag-tsam.*" Just me. Just the little old Dalai Lama.

I interpret that as the third stage in a process of thinking that leads us initially from our naïve affirmation of the conventional categories of ordinary experience, through a very hard-nosed and analytical philosophically accurate and philosophically intense scrutiny of the reality of different aspects of experience, and then at the end brings us back to the conventional world. One way to think about this is to think that that third stage in the process of reasoning is something like the realization that Emptiness itself is empty. We pursue Emptiness as doctrine from ordinary experience, a realization that takes us out of the illusions of this world. Then, we have to realize that that view of Emptiness itself is empty. It brings us back to an appreciation of our conventional experience and allows us to sit with a certain quality of freedom and attention within the conventional world with which we began. This is a very common process of reasoning in the Mahayana, a process that starts with conventionality; pursues a radical, critical appreciation of the doctrine of Emptiness; and then returns to conventional experience with the same sense of lightness and freedom that the Dalai Lama expressed with that simple phrase, "Who am I? Just me." Just self.

I think sometimes that in all of the complexities of Buddhist philosophy, and we could by looking at the many different traditions of interpretation of the Emptiness doctrine spend much complexity, the most important thing to hold onto is simply the simplicity of that final comment, that final phrase. "Who is the self? Just me." Just the conventional world stripped of any imputation of ultimate reality.

The philosophical implication of the doctrine of Emptiness leads us into a doctrine of two truths. Finally, what was the institutional outcome of the doctrine of Emptiness? In Tibet in particular, the doctrine of Emptiness gave rise to a very sophisticated and complex tradition of philosophical study. Some people sometimes ask me when we talk about Buddhist monasticism, "What do Buddhist monks do when they're not out begging for their food in the morning or engaging in acts of worship or meditation?" In the Tibetan tradition in particular, one of the things that they do is to study quite intensively the philosophical traditions that grew up around this doctrine of Emptiness. Emptiness became the basis and intellectual focus of a complex and sophisticated tradition of monastic education, particularly in Tibet.

All of that took place, you might say, within the mainstream of the Mahayana. All of that belongs to the tradition of bodhisattva practice and discipline we've been talking about in our earlier lectures. There's another, perhaps even more striking, expression of the Emptiness doctrine that appeared in a tradition that's known as Buddhist Tantra. Tantric Buddhism began to emerge in India during the sixth century of the Common Era. I use the word "emerge" here quite deliberately, because we don't really know exactly where it came from. Its origin, like the origin of many important teachings in Indian Buddhism, is quite obscure. It emerged very clearly into historical consciousness during the sixth century of the Common Era.

Tantra is known by a couple of different names that are worth knowing about so that you can identify it when you come across it in the Buddhist traditions of the world. First of all, it's called the "*Vajrayana*," which means the "Diamond Vehicle." It's a vehicle that brings you to a state of awakening that is as hard as a diamond and as sharp as a thunderbolt. It's also called the *Mantrayana*, the "Vehicle of Powerful Words," because mantras, like that mantra that's used to invoke the compassion of Avalokiteshvara, are particularly widely used in the tradition of Buddhist Tantra.

The term *Tantra* itself, incidentally, is a puzzling artifact in the tradition. It can have many different meanings. The fundamental meaning, the one out of which others seem to arise is simply the meaning that's associated with the warp on a weaver's loom over which the weft is woven. The Tantra refers, as it were, to the warp of reality on which the rest of experience is woven. Tantra can also be used to refer to power because the Tantric tradition often has to do with the acquisition and development of power. It can refer to the lineage of transmission that moves from teacher to disciple. That, too, is important in Tantric practice and Tantric tradition.

How then is the Tantric tradition related to earlier forms of Buddhism? Sometimes people say that Tantra is a separate vehicle alongside the Hinayana and the Mahayana. It's probably more helpful and more accurate to consider Tantra as an extension of the values of the Mahayana, particularly the value and the concept of non-duality. In the Tantric tradition, the concept of non-duality is taken to an extraordinary and radical extreme. We can see this probably most visibly in the concept of the Buddha, the image of the Buddha that was developed and used in Tantric devotion.

The Buddha that we know, the Buddha that we've been talking about now for several lectures, was a serene and a peaceful figure. In fact, it wasn't so long ago that we visualized the serenity of the Buddha and tried to seek his help as an antidote to all of the confusion and anger and buzzing distraction that appears as we're trying to commute in the morning through rush-hour traffic. The Buddha for us is that kind of image of serenity and quiet contemplation.

In the Tantric tradition, the Buddha came to be visualized not just as a serene figure, but as a figure full of passion and wrath. This is the classic Tantric image of a wrathful Buddha with bulging eyes and fangs and wild hair, dancing on the corpses of his enemies, an extraordinary figure of the Buddha marking for us a radical change in the image of what Buddha-hood involves. Why would they picture the Buddha this way? First of all, simply to re-emphasize for us that there is in the end no ultimate distinction between the image of the Buddha as wrath, and the image of the Buddha as serene contemplation. Tantric texts talk about this, not just in relation to the Buddha himself, but also in the relation to Tantric practice. It's possible to meditate on one's emotions, particularly one's negative emotions, in a way that transmutes them into experiences of enlightenment.

Let me read a short passage that indicates the significance of this in Tantric terminology: "Those who do not perceive the truth think in terms of samsara and nirvana. But those who perceive the truth, think neither of samsara, nor of nirvana. Discriminating thought, then, is the great demon that produces the ocean of samsara, but being free of this discriminating thought, the great ones are freed from the bonds of existence. Just as water that has entered the ear may be removed by water, and just as a thorn may be removed by a thorn, so those who know remove passion by means of passion itself. Just as a washerman removes the grime from a garment by means of grime, so the wise person renders himself free of impurity by means of impurity itself."

The Tantric tradition uses images of impurity, of anger, of passion, wrath—all those states of emotion and states of mind that, in the earlier tradition, would've been considered barriers to awakening—and uses them as meditative means to understand the experience of non-duality.

In the Tantric tradition, Buddhas can be pictured not just as wrathful figures, but also as images of the union of male and female. What more fundamental duality in human experience is there than this? The Tantric tradition is seeking a direct appreciation of non-duality. Why not visualize the Buddha, not just as a male figure, but as the union of male and female in intimate embrace? These figures are known in Tibetan tradition as *yab-yum* images, from the Tibetan word that means "male and female" or "father and mother." I suspect that many of you have seen them in museums. It's a very common form of Buddha image, especially in the Tibetan tradition.

People often ask when they see these yab-yum images, whether they were meant to be taken literally and to suggest that sexual union is some form of Buddha-hood. This question actually is difficult to answer because the texts are not always easy to interpret. There's no question in some situations, in some levels of Tantric practice, that a ritual of sexual union did play a role in Tantric meditation. It's more common for these images to function as symbolic representations of a mind that has transcended all dualities, including the distinction between the sexes.

We have two classic images of non-duality in Buddhist Tantra: The image of the Buddha as a wrathful figure, and the image of the Buddha as the union of male and female. You can see here that the theme underlying both of these images is a unification of opposites. To discern places where Buddha-hood has been associated with one thing as opposed to another, and then to achieve by some kind of symbolic representation the unification of those two opposites in an experience of non-duality. There are other ways of doing this in Tantric tradition as well.

One of the most important is the representation of the Buddha and the representation of all of reality in the image of a sacred circle, or a *mandala*. A basic mandala, sacred circle, contains the images of four Buddhas, located at each of the cardinal directions—North, South, East, and West—with a fifth Buddha in the center, who represents ultimate reality. In Tantric ritual—in the ritual practice of the mandala, and in meditation guided by the structure of the mandala—practitioners learn to unify their own personalities as if they themselves, in their own person-hood, were miniature mandalas with a mandala of the five Buddhas as a ritual object, and through that mandala, with a mandala of the universe as a whole.

The form of the mandala achieves a unification of thought and of reality for a Tantric practitioner by unifying the mandala of the personality. Think of it perhaps as the mandala in microcosm, with the mandala of the ritual object, the mandala of the five Buddhas—call this perhaps a mesocosm—the cosmos that stands in the middle, and through that, with the cosmos in the largest sense possible, the macrocosm. All of reality visualized as if it, too, were a mandala, a sacred circle with the four cardinal directions, with a central figure of the Buddha sitting right in the middle. The mandala is extremely important in Tantric ritual, in Tantric symbolism, and in Tantric practice, not just in India, but in all the places where the Tantric tradition moved and then flourished—in Tibet, in China, and in Japan. It's used as a form of visualization in order to make offerings to the deity and to come to understand your own relationship to the cosmos in a deeper way. It can also be understood, interestingly enough, even as a guide for pilgrimage because Tibet as a sacred land is constructed in the form of a mandala. You can do pilgrimage in Tibet by moving around the shrines that mark the perimeter of Tibet and then passing to the center of the mandala that sits in the capital city of Tibet, the City of Lhasa.

All of these different aspects of the Tantric tradition grow, as you can see, out of the fundamental insight of the doctrine of Emptiness, and have to be understood—for us as beginning students of Buddhism—as one more striking, bold manifestation of the religious impulse that gave rise to the Mahayana tradition itself.

Lecture Nine
Theravada Buddhism in Southeast Asia

Scope:

During the reign of the Buddhist king Asoka (c. 269–238 B.C.E.), the first Buddhist missionaries left India for Sri Lanka. From this missionary effort grew the *Theravada* ("Tradition of the Elders") Buddhism that now dominates all the Buddhist countries of Southeast Asia except Vietnam. Along with Asoka's missionaries came the Buddhist concept of a "righteous king," exemplified by Asoka himself. Throughout the history of Theravada Buddhism in Southeast Asia, there has been a close relationship between the Buddhist Samgha and Buddhist political leaders. This relationship is evident in Thailand, where Buddhist kings have played a key role in the reform and revitalization of the Buddhist Samgha. It also plays a role in the work of Aung San Suu Kyi, who won the 1991 Nobel Peace Prize for her nonviolent resistance to military authority in Burma.

Outline

I. In the last few lectures, we have seen that Buddhism in India changed substantially in the centuries that followed the Buddha's death.

    A. This process of change continued until about the year 1200, when a series of Muslim invasions destroyed the major monasteries in North India and effectively brought the history of Indian Buddhism to an end.

    B. To continue the story of Buddhism, we now have to shift our attention to the history of Buddhist sectarianism outside India.

    C. After the death of the Buddha, disputes in the Samgha generated a series of sectarian movements known as *nikayas*.

    D. Most of these sects are now only historical artifacts, but one is still active: the *Theravada* ("Doctrine of the Elders") tradition of Southeast Asia.

II. This lecture will explore the history of Theravada Buddhism.

    A. One way to study the Theravada tradition would be to focus on the history of Buddhist monasticism in Southeast Asia. This tradition is quite strong and sophisticated.

1. Buddhaghosa, the great commentator on the Pali canon, systematized the doctrine of Therevada Buddhism.
2. Forest monks keep alive the ascetical traditions of primitive Buddhism.

B. To study the tradition anthropologically, we could focus on the way Buddhist values have been interwoven with the popular cults of spirits and ghosts. There is such a deep connection between Buddhism and popular spirit cults in the Theravada world that it often is difficult to draw the line between Buddhism and popular religion. Some interpreters say that there is not even a line to draw.

C. In our brief discussion of Therevada Buddhism, we will focus on the relationship between Buddhism and politics.

III. This story starts with King Asoka, who reigned from 269 to 238 B.C.E. and became the prototype of a Buddhist "righteous king" (*dhamma-raja*). Traditional chronicles report that his son was the first Buddhist missionary to Sri Lanka.

A. When King Asoka assumed the throne in 269 B.C.E. as emperor of the Maurya Dynasty, he waged a bloody campaign to conquer a small kingdom known as Kalinga. The brutality of this campaign provoked Asoka to convert to Buddhism.
1. After his conversion, Asoka proclaimed himself a "righteous king" (*dhamma-raja*), or protector of the Dharma, and advocated a policy of conquest by Dharma (*dhamma-vijaya*) rather than by force of arms.
2. Asoka's position was recorded in a series of Rock Edicts placed at strategic spots around his empire.
3. Rock Edict XIII gives an account of his conversion:

Eight years after his coronation, King Devanampriya Priyadarshi [Asoka] conquered Kalinga. One hundred and fifty thousand persons were deported, one hundred thousand were killed, and many times that number perished. Now that the Kalingans have been taken, Devanampriya is zealous in his study of Dharma. Devanampriya feels sorrow at having conquered the Kalingans... Indeed, Devanampriya wishes all beings to be safe, restrained, and even-keeled in the face of violence. For Devanampriya considers the foremost form of conquest to be Dharma-conquest.

From John S. Strong, *The Experience of Buddhism: Sources and Interpretations* (Belmont, CA: Wadsworth, 1995), pp. 84–85.

4. Other Rock Edicts describe Asoka's policy of promoting the Dharma:

    King Devanampriya Priyadarshi says: I have had banyan trees planted along the roads to provide shade for beasts and people, and I have had mango groves planted. And I have had wells dug and rest areas built every mile, and here and there I have had watering holes made for the enjoyment of beasts and humans.... Of course, previous kings as well have sought to please the people with such facilities, but I am doing this so that people may follow the path of Dharma.

    From John S. Strong, *The Experience of Buddhism: Sources and Interpretations* (Belmont, CA: Wadsworth, 1995), p. 85.

B. Tradition tells us that Asoka sent out missionaries to spread the Buddha's teaching. His actions have continued to serve as a model for "righteous kings" throughout the Buddhist world.
    1. A righteous king protects and promulgates the Dharma. In return, the king is recognized or "legitimated" by the religious authority of the monks.
    2. In some situations, the king disciplines and reforms the Samgha to make sure that it adheres to proper discipline and does not interfere in the affairs of the state.
    3. Asoka himself set an example for the control and discipline of the Samgha when he said: "Any monk or nun who causes a schism in the Samgha will have to wear the white robes of a layperson and will no longer be able to dwell in a monastic residence. This order should be made known to both the community of monks and the community of nuns... and a copy of this edict shall be given to the laity" (Strong, p. 85).

IV. One of the most striking examples of a "righteous king" in modern Southeast Asia is King Rama IV or King Mongkut of Thailand.

    A. King Mongkut (r. 1851–1868) spent 25 years as a monk, then, as king, instituted a reform movement to modernize Thai monastic life.

        1. As king, Mongkut believed that Thai monastic life needed to be purged of "superstitious" practices and returned to the pristine model of the Pali canon.

        2. He gave institutional form to his ideas by creating the Thammayut movement.

        3. During the reign of his son, King Chulalongkorn (1868–1910), this reform movement was extended throughout the Thai Samgha and given the status of an official orthodoxy and a national religion.

    B. Thailand continues to be an example of the close alliance between king and Samgha. Important symbols of the connection between royal power and Buddhist practice in Bangkok include the Temple of the Emerald Buddha, where the central image functions not just as a focus of worship, but as a symbol of Thai national identity and the legitimacy of the royal family.

V. Aung San Suu Kyi of Myanmar (Burma), a democratic activist and Nobel laureate, gives another example of the intersection between religious and political values in Southeast Asia.

    A. Aung San Suu Kyi was born in 1945 as the daughter of Burma's national hero General Aung San. Her father led the Burmese liberation movement during World War II. He was assassinated in 1947, just before Burma gained its independence.

    B. Aung San Suu Kyi was educated in Rangoon, Delhi, and Oxford and settled down to raise a family in Oxford, until she was called back to Burma by her mother's illness in 1988.

    C. In Burma, she became involved in a spontaneous revolt against 26 years of repressive military rule. She soon emerged as the movement's leader.

        1. Even though she was placed under house arrest, her movement won a colossal electoral victory in May 1990.

2. The military government annulled the results of the election and imprisoned its leaders.

3. Aung San Suu Kyi has continued to speak out in support of the democratic movement.

D. In 1991, she received the Nobel Peace Prize and was cited by the Nobel committee "for her unflagging efforts... for democracy, human rights, and ethnic conciliation by peaceful means."

E. Aung San Suu Kyi's political philosophy seems, on the face of it, to be quite simple and straightforward. But her words carry force and eloquence that echo teachings of the Buddha.

1. One of her most famous speeches is called simply "Freedom from Fear." She begins the speech by saying: "It is not power that corrupts but fear. Fear of losing power corrupts those who wield it and fear of the scourge of power corrupts those who are subject to it" (Aung San Suu Kyi, *Freedom from Fear and Other Writings* [London: Penguin, 1991]).

2. Near the end of the speech, she refers to Mahatma Gandhi's statement that the greatest gift for an individual or a nation is fearlessness, "not merely bodily courage, but absence of fear from the mind." (This refers to a story about the Buddha's gesture of fearlessness when he was threatened by a raging elephant.)

3. Aung San Suu Kyi adds her own Buddhist twist to Gandhi's words by saying, "Fearlessness may be a gift but perhaps more precious is the courage acquired through endeavor, courage that cultivates the habit of refusing to let fear dictate one's actions."

F. Anyone who listens to these words can hear how Aung San Suu Kyi's career brings together modern democratic values and the fundamental Buddhist values of courage, patience, tolerance, and nonviolence. It is a powerful mix for anyone who wonders whether Buddhist values belong only in the monastery. Here, they play a forceful and active role in political life.

VI. Shifting from Myanmar to Sri Lanka, we find a political situation that is even more problematic.

A. Sri Lanka has been torn apart for more than a decade by a bloody ethnic conflict between Tamil Hindus and Sri Lankan Buddhists.

    1. One of the most puzzling aspects of this conflict for those who think of Buddhism as a peaceful religion is the way Buddhist monks have sometimes used Buddhist tradition to fan the flames of conflict.

    2. Scholars who study this struggle trace its roots to the colonial period, when Buddhist leaders appealed to the island's Buddhist identity as a way of mobilizing resistance to the British colonial administration. Buddhism came to be the defining characteristic of Sri Lanka as a nation.

    3. When the British left, Sri Lanka was given the opportunity to establish itself as a Buddhist community. The problem was that large portions of the country, especially in the north, were Hindu minority communities. The struggle for power between Buddhists and Hindus produced a bloody conflict that continues today.

B. Sri Lanka is a case where the political impact of Buddhist values has not been entirely benign.

Essential Reading:

Robinson and Johnson, *The Buddhist Religion*, ch. 7.

Supplementary Reading:

Strong, *The Experience of Buddhism*, ch. 6.

Aung San Suu Kyi, *Freedom from Fear and Other Writings*.

Questions to Consider:

1. Some historians have questioned whether Asoka's dhamma really was Buddhism in any recognizable sense. What is "Buddhist" about his imperial ideology?

2. Why do you think Asoka found the Buddha's teaching attractive as a political strategy?

3. Aung San Suu Kyi's speeches are widely available on the Internet. (You can search for them under her name.) What is Buddhist about her political program?

Lecture Nine—Transcript
Theravada Buddhism in Southeast Asia

In the last few lectures, we've seen that Buddhism in India changed pretty substantially in the centuries that followed the Buddha's death. This process of change continued until about the year 1200, when a series of Muslim invasions from Afghanistan moved down across northern India and destroyed the major monasteries that had really been the center of Buddhist culture in northern India for many centuries. They effectively brought the history of Indian Buddhism to an end. For us to continue the story of Buddhism, we have to shift our attention to the changes that took place outside India. We'll begin this lecture talking about the Buddhism of Southeast Asia.

You may recall that in our discussion of the history of the Buddhist Samgha, right after the death of the Buddha, I said that, about a hundred years after the Buddha's parinirvana, the disputes in the Samgha, disputes inside the Buddhist community, generated a series of sectarian movements that we know now as the *nikayas*, the sects of traditional Buddhism. Most of these sectarian movements are now just historical artifacts, but one is still active. This is the *Theravada* tradition, the "Doctrine of the Elders" that is practiced throughout Southeast Asia.

There are lots of ways for us to study the Theravada tradition. It is a long, rich, and historically complex tradition. It would be possible for us to spend more than the half hour we have just talking about Buddhist monasticism in Southeast Asia. There is one great figure, for example, by the name of Buddhaghosa, who stepped in in Sri Lanka at a certain period and codified the tradition of commentaries on the Pali canon, and provided what you might consider the scholastic super structure of Theravada Buddhism. Buddhaghosa, himself, is a marvelous figure and would be well worth studying.

It also would be interesting for us to spend some time talking about the tradition of forest monks in Southeast Asia. These are people that kept alive the ascetic tradition of the Buddha, living often in forest hermitages, and became the focus of a certain rather intense devotion amongst Buddhist laypeople in Southeast Asia.

It's also worth knowing, I think in passing, that social anthropologists have studied the Buddhist traditions of Southeast Asia in a particularly rich and interesting way, and have shown how much Buddhist values have interacted with—and become intermingled with—the tradition of worship and veneration of local ghosts and spirits so much so that it's now difficult to draw the line between values that are distinctively Buddhist and values that are associated with indigenous religious traditions in Southeast Asia. In fact, in many cases, it's unclear that there really is a line to draw. All of these would be topics that would be well worth spending some time on. In fact, in the time we've got, I think it's important for us to focus instead on another crucial issue that will lead us into a dimension of Buddhism that really has not been very visible in the lectures that we've had so far. This has to do with the relationship between Buddhist monks and Buddhist kings, the interaction between the tradition of Buddhist monasticism and the whole complex super structure of political leadership that has been so important in the development of Buddhism throughout Southeast Asia.

To tell this story, to focus on this aspect of Buddhism, we begin not with contemporary Southeast Asia, but with a crucial Buddhist king who became the model for Buddhist kingship in subsequent generations. His name is King Asoka. He reigned in India from the year 269 to 238 Before the Common Era. He became the prototype of the "righteous king," or the *dhamma-raja*, in Buddhist tradition. When King Asoka assumed the throne in 269, B.C.E., as Emperor of the Maurya Dynasty, which is really the first great dynasty that unified large portions of northern India, he waged a bloody campaign to conquer a small, nearby kingdom over on the eastern side of India known as Kalinga.

According to the traditions that are told about Asoka, some of them going back to Asoka himself, this campaign was so bloody and so cruel that it provoked Asoka to convert to Buddhism and to adopt a strategy of nonviolence. After his conversion, Asoka proclaimed himself a "righteous king," a *dhamma-raja*, a king who is associated in some way with the protection of the Dhamma or the Dharma. He advocated a policy of conquest by Dharma, rather than by force of arms. Asoka's position was recorded in a serious of rock edicts that were carved in the rock and placed at strategic spots in his empire. I'll read you a couple of these just to give you a sense of how Asoka, himself, presented his own Dharma, his own imperial policy and his own understanding of Buddhism.

Rock Edict 13 gives a really intriguing account of Asoka's conversion, at least how it tells us he may have visualized it himself. Eight years after his coronation, King Devanampriya Priyadarshi, that is King Asoka, conquered Kalinga. One hundred and fifty thousand persons were deported. One hundred thousand were killed. These seem like extraordinarily large numbers, but perhaps they're accurate. Many times that number perished. Now that the Kalingans had been taken, Devanampriya is zealous in his study of Dharma. Devanampriya feels sorrow at having conquered the Kalingans. Indeed, Devanampriya wishes all beings to be safe, restrained, and even keeled in the face of violence, for Devanampriya considers the foremost form of conquest to be Dharma conquests, conquest by the truth and by the teaching of nonviolence.

Other rock edicts describe Asoka's policy to promote the Dharma. King Devanampriya says, "I have had banyan trees planted along the roads to provide shade for beasts and people, and I have had mango groves planted, and I have had wells dug and rest areas built every mile, and here and there I have had watering holes made for the enjoyment of beasts and humans." It sounds like a marvelous place to be, actually. "Of course, previous kings, as well, have sought to please the people with such facilities, but I am doing this so that the people may follow the path of Dharma." You'd be hard-pressed here, to see anything in this that's distinctively Buddhist. Yet, Asoka clearly associated this policy of peaceful promoting of public welfare in his kingdom as being a Buddhist strategy to encourage loyalty and support among his people and also, not incidentally, to simply provide a better life for the people who lived in his kingdom.

Tradition tells us that Asoka sent out missionaries to spread the Buddha's teaching, not just around northern India, but elsewhere in India and across the seas. His actions have served as a model for so-called righteous kings throughout the Buddhist world. A righteous king protects and promulgates the Dharma and, in return, the king is recognized, or as sociologists of religion sometimes say, legitimated by the support, sometimes in ritual form, sometimes merely by verbal support, from the monasteries. In some situations, the king actually disciplines and reforms the Samgha, to make sure that it adheres to proper discipline and doesn't interfere in the affairs of the state. The support and influence runs in both directions.

Asoka himself set an example for the control and for the discipline of the Samgha when he said, "Any monk or nun who causes a schism in the Samgha will have to wear the white robes of a layperson." In other words, they'll be stripped of their monastic identity and will no longer be able to dwell in a monastic residence. This order should be made known to both the community of monks and the community of nuns. A copy of this edict should also be given to the laity so the laity can watch out for this kind of disobedient behavior amongst the monks and the nuns. Asoka set in motion a very important historical example that has served as a model for Buddhist kings for the last couple of millennia, not merely in India, but also in the other countries where Buddhism has spread.

One of the most striking examples of a righteous king in modern Southeast Asian history is King Rama IV or King Mongkut of Thailand. King Mongkut reigned from 1851 to 1868, not so long ago, in the middle of the 19th century. He spent 25 years as a monk before becoming a king. When he became a king, he instituted a reform movement to modernize Thai monastic life. As a king, he believed that the Thai monastic organization needed to be reformed and purged of superstitious practices and returned to the pristine model of the Pali canon.

If this seems just a little bit like movements that you've encountered in other religious traditions in the last hundred years or so, it's not entirely by accident. You know that part of being a religious person in encounter with the modern world is to attempt to take your tradition, as rich and complex and full of legendary accretions as it may be, and attempt to make it consistent with the modern view of the world.

Thomas Jefferson, for example, just to pick a rather interesting modernist who was close to home, felt, in reading the Bible, that all the miraculous experiences that were associated with Jesus, all of the great healing miracles and so on and so forth, were, for him, a barrier to understanding Christianity. He produced a document that's known as the "Jefferson Bible" in which he extracted the miraculous elements of the gospel narrative and left us with the moral teaching because, for him, Jesus was an influential, wise teacher about how to live a good life. What he hoped to do was to remove the element of the miraculous and the superstitious from the image of Jesus and simply focus on the moral teaching of Jesus himself.

This is exactly the kind of thing that King Mongkut tried to do in Thailand. He tried to filter out of monastic practice and monastic teaching a lot of, what he called, superstitious practices or what were understood, in that time, to be superstitious practices—having to do with supernatural beings of one sort or another—and focus on the moral and ethical teachings of the Pali canon. King Mongkut is, for us, a classic example of a Buddhist modernist and reformer. What's particularly remarkable about him is that he's not merely a modernist, of which we have many examples, but he was a king and a monk. He had the knowledge and the authority to bring these reforms to reality.

He gave institutional form to his ideas by creating a movement known as the Thammayut Movement in the Thai Samgha during the reign of his son, King Chulalongkorn, who reigned from 1868 to 1910, bringing the Thai royal family and the Thai monastic organization into the 20th Century. This reform movement was extended throughout the Thai Samgha. It was given the status of official orthodoxy and also the status of a national religion. It became the orthodox teaching of the Samgha. It also was associated with the identity of Thailand as a Buddhist nation. Thailand continues to be an example of the close alliance between king and Samgha in the extension and protection of Buddhist values in its place where one can go now to see this ancient pattern of reciprocity and mutual support and criticism still being worked out today.

Important symbols of the connection between royal power and Buddhist practice in Bangkok include the Temple of the Emerald Buddha, a shrine that would be well worth visiting if you haven't had a chance to visit it already. The central image in the Temple of the Emerald Buddha is a rather small Buddha surrounded by an extraordinarily complex and beautiful shrine. This central image functions not just as a focus of worship. Obviously people come there and pay their respects to the Buddha by worshipping the image, but it has become a symbol of Thai national identity and also embodies and encapsulates, in a certain remarkable way, the legitimacy of the Thai Royal Family. The power of kingship is associated in this culture with the legitimacy of the practice of Buddhism, itself.

If we shift our attention from Thailand to Burma, or to as it is now called, to Myanmar, we see a different example of the relationship between Buddhism and political life, not the relationship between monk and king, but the relationship between Buddhist values and the very powerful and very significant movement of contemporary, democratic reform. Burma's most famous political dissident, Aung San Suu Kyi, was born in 1945 as the daughter of Burma's national hero, General Aung San. Her father led the Burmese Liberation Movement during World War II and was assassinated in 1947, just before Burma gained its independence.

Aung San Suu Kyi was educated first in Rangoon, then she moved on to Delhi and, finally, she moved on to Oxford for her higher education. She married a Buddhist scholar in Oxford whose name was Michael Aris. He was a very wonderful scholar of Bhutanese Buddhism and a remarkably fine human being. With Michael, she settled down to raise a family in Oxford until she was called back to Burma by her mother's illness in 1988. In Burma, she became involved, I think accidentally at first, in what became a spontaneous democratic revolt against 26 years of repressive military rule in Burma. Soon, because of her eloquence and her presence and her connection with her very famous father, she emerged as the movement's leader.

The movement eventually won a colossal electoral victory in May 1990. The military government annulled the results of the election and imprisoned its leaders. When she was under house arrest, Aung San Suu Kyi continued to speak out in favor of democracy in Burma. In 1991, she received the Nobel Peace Prize and was cited by the Nobel Committee for what they called, "her unflagging efforts for democracy, human rights, and ethic conciliation by peaceful means."

Aung San Suu Kyi's political philosophy seems, on the face of it, to be pretty simple, but there is a force and eloquence in her words and always subtle echo of the teaching of the Buddha. One of her most famous speeches is called simply, "Freedom from Fear." The speech begins by saying, "It's not power that corrupts, but fear. Fear of losing power corrupts those who wield it and fear of the scourge of power corrupts those who are subject to it." Near the end of her speech she refers to Mahatma Gandhi's statement that the greatest gift for an individual or for a nation is fearlessness, not merely, as she says, "bodily courage," but "absence of fear from the mind."

This is simple: fearlessness, courage. What more fundamental political virtues could there be than this? It hardly seems that there's any thing distinctively Buddhist about this. Yet, if you think back to some of the classic images of the Buddha, especially the gestures of the Buddha that are represented very commonly in Buddhist art, we've talked about one of them. It was that Earth-touching gesture in which the Buddha reached down with one of his hands and touched the Earth to bear witness to the strength of his meditation.

There is another gesture, very common in Buddhist art that we haven't talked about. It's sometimes referred to by students as "the great traffic cop" gesture where the Buddha reaches out like this and seems to be stopping traffic in a busy intersection. He's got his hand up above his shoulder and seems to be stopping a line of cars. It actually comes from a story told about the Buddha's life when a figure in a monastery who was causing a revolt attempted to attack the Buddha by luring him into a narrow lane and then turning a wild elephant loose in the lane to run the Buddha over. The elephant came charging down the street. The name of the elephant is told in the story, but I can't remember exactly what it is at this moment. In any case, the elephant is racing down the lane. The Buddha, walking forward slowly as he seems to do in these stories, simply holds out his arm in "the great traffic cop" gesture, the great gesture of fearlessness. The elephant screeches to a halt and bows down and pays him homage. It's a wonderful image in Buddhist art.

One of the most basic gestures that the Buddha performs, at least in the Buddhist artistic tradition, is to give the gift of fearlessness, simply to hold out his hand and to allow you in some way to imbibe some of the fearlessness and confidence of the Buddha himself. Professors usually don't have the same kind of charismatic presence, I would have to say, as the Buddha. If I could be the Buddha, perhaps I wouldn't even be a professor. Who knows? In any case, there are a few moments in the ordinary flow of the year when the gift of fearlessness is not a bad thing to dispense to people who need it. I often have undergraduates who come racing into my office and say, "Oh, my God, Professor, I just don't know how I'm going to be able to do on this examination that we have coming up next week. I'm so confused. I don't know how to study for it. What can I do?"

Chances are, there are other things that are occupying one's attention at that moment. You can't actually sit down and review an entire course with someone to prepare them for the exam. What I often do is say, "Well, listen Peter, listen Grace, take from me the gift of fearlessness." Just like the gift of fearlessness that the Buddha gave to his community in that basic gesture that's represented in Buddhist art. As often as not, perhaps this is my imagination, people leave the office feeling a sense of confidence and fearlessness. This is the idea that Aung San Suu Kyi made the key to her political philosophy in Burma. It's a simple gesture, it's a simple idea, and yet it grows right out of the strength and confidence of the Buddhist tradition itself.

Aung San Suu Kyi explicitly adds a Buddhist twist to these words by saying, "Fearlessness may be a gift, but perhaps more precious is the courage acquired through endeavor, courage that cultivates the habit of refusing to let fear dictate one's actions." Political activity, for her, is an expression of a certain kind of Buddhist attitude and mind based on confidence and on fearlessness. Anyone who listens to these words can hear how Aung San Suu Kyi's career brings together modern democratic values and the fundamental Buddhist values of courage, patience, tolerance, and nonviolence. It's a powerful mix for anyone who wonders whether Buddhist values belong only in a monastery. Here they play a very forceful and active role in political life.

As I'm speaking today, Aung San Suu Kyi has recently been released from detention. Many people are hopeful that she'll be able to play a strong and very positive role in leading Burma through what we hope will be a transition to democracy.

In this discussion of political life in Southeast Asia, I haven't said anything at all about Sri Lanka, the country that, in many respects, has been the homeland, the spawning ground of Theravada Buddhism throughout Southeast Asia. What's the situation in Sri Lanka politically and religiously? It's actually even more problematic than the situation in Burma. Sri Lanka has been torn apart for more than a decade by a bloody ethnic conflict between Tamil Hindus and Sri Lankan Buddhists. One of the most puzzling aspects of this conflict, for those of us who think of Buddhism as being a peaceful, tolerant, and nonviolent religion, is the way Buddhist monks have sometimes used Buddhist tradition and a sense of Buddhist identity to feed the flames of the conflict.

Scholars, who study this struggle, trace its origins to the colonial period when Buddhist leaders appealed to the island's Buddhist identity as a way of mobilizing resistance to the British Colonial administration. Buddhism came to be the defining characteristic of

Sri Lanka as a nation. You may have encountered this in other traditions in South Asia in your study of Great Religions of the World. One of the most important things that happened in many countries that were subject to colonial rule was a constant pressing of the question, "What is it that makes us a nation that is proud, distinctive, and can stand up to the colonial domination of the European powers? This is an extremely important question in India in the 19th century and gave rise to some very significant movements, not the least of which eventually, of course, was the movement that Mahatma Gandhi crystallized that eventually produced the independence of India.

This question was posed in Sri Lanka, as well, but it was given a Buddhist form, since Sri Lanka is a Buddhist country. A number of people whose names I won't mention, but who were important leaders in the tradition in this time, said that Buddhism was really the core of Sri Lankan identity and could be used, as it were, as an ideological platform to establish the independence of Sri Lanka and to drive out the foreign administration that had imposed its power on the Sri Lankan community.

Eventually, of course, this was a successful struggle. After the Second World War, the British colonial forces left Sri Lanka as they left India and left other parts of the world. Sri Lanka was given the opportunity to establish itself as a Buddhist culture with its own traditions and its own sense of national identity. The problem was that Sri Lanka was not an entirely Buddhist country. In portions of Sri Lanka, particularly in the north, there were large Hindu Tamil ethnic minority communities. In the struggle for political power in Sri Lanka, immense tensions began to develop between the Sri Lankan Buddhists on the one side and Tamil Hindus on the other, resulting, eventually, in a bloody ethnic insurgency led by a group known as the Tamil Tigers attempting to establish the independence of the Tamil homeland in northern Sri Lanka. Since that time, the two groups have fought back and forth in a vicious ethnic conflict.

To make a long story short, the Buddhists in Sri Lanka began to appeal to their Buddhist identity and Buddhist values to give justification for their struggle against the Tamil minority. They looked back into Sri Lankan tradition to a chronicle known as the Mahavamsa that traced this ancient ethnic struggle back 2,000 years to the time when Buddhism was first introduced to this island nation.

Whether Buddhists in Sri Lanka will be able to re-appropriate some of the peaceful, nonviolent, and tolerant aspects of the tradition, as well, and to use these as a way of settling this terrible conflict is as yet unknown. I think those of us who are standing now as observers and students of the Buddhist tradition have to realize that, at least, in this one particular case, Buddhist values have had political impact that has not been entirely benign.

It shows how complex it is to study, discuss, and make some sense of this troubled and problematic way in which religious values interact with political culture. In many respects, Buddhism has had a very positive, benign, peaceful, and tolerant effect on the political life of Southeast Asia, but we know from the present situation in Sri Lanka, that this does not always have to be the case. The political struggle, I would have to say, simply continues for the soul of Buddhism in Southeast Asia.

Lecture Ten
Buddhism in Tibet

Scope:

The "First Diffusion" of the Dharma in Tibet began in the seventh century when the Tibetan king Songtsen Gampo built a temple in Lhasa to house an image of the Buddha. The early history of Tibetan Buddhism was shaped by models borrowed from India. The Indian saint Padmasambhava, or Guru Rinpoche, gave Tibetan Buddhism a strong Tantric flavor, and Shantarakshita introduced Tibetans to the intellectual traditions of the Indian monasteries. Eventually, Tibetan Buddhists developed a tradition of four schools: the Nyingma, Sakya, Kagyu, and Geluk—each with is own distinctive characteristics. Today, the Tibetan tradition is best known in the figure of the 14th Dalai Lama, recipient of the Nobel Peace Prize in 1989 for his peaceful campaign of resistance to Chinese domination in Tibet.

Outline

I. In the latter half of the first millennium C.E. (from about 600 to 1200 C.E.), the teachings of the Mahayana and the ritual practices of Tantra were absorbed into the sophisticated intellectual life of the Indian Buddhist monasteries.

    A. These monasteries had large libraries, colorful rituals, and an elaborate monastic curriculum, ranging all the way from Buddhist philosophy and meditation to astronomy and medicine. Unfortunately, their cultural strength turned out to be their greatest weakness.

        1. When waves of Afghan raiders began to sweep across the Ganges Basin, the monasteries were tempting targets for plunder and destruction.

        2. By the year 1200, after two centuries of persecution, there was little left of Buddhist monastic culture but a handful of destitute, old monks.

    B. We now trace the Mahayana tradition beyond the Himalayas to Tibet, where Indian monastic culture has been preserved more faithfully and more richly than anywhere else in the Buddhist world.

II. The "First Diffusion" of the Dharma in Tibet began in the seventh century.

A. During the seventh century, a line of kings in central Tibet united the Tibetan tribes and began to extend their military influence outside the Tibetan plateau. As they turned their attention beyond Tibet, they encountered the lively Buddhist cultures of India, Nepal, China, and Central Asia.

B. According to Tibetan tradition, King Songtsen Gampo (c. 609–49) invited one of his two Buddhist wives to help him introduce the cult of the Buddha to Tibet.

    1. The initial attempts to build a temple in the capital of Lhasa were unsuccessful.

    2. In a dream, the king was told that the land of Tibet lay on the body of a demoness who had to be subdued before the cult of the Buddha could be successfully established.

    3. He ordered a series of temples to be built around the country, pinning down her knees and elbows and her hips and shoulders. Finally, a temple was built in Lhasa to pin down her heart.

    4. This temple is the Jokhang, the most sacred temple in Tibet and the site of the Jobo Rinpoche, Songtsen Gampo's first Buddha image.

C. The actions of Songtsen Gampo not only subdued the demoness that was Tibet, but they marked Tibet with the form of a mandala.

D. During this early period in Tibetan Buddhist history, Tibetans fixed the spelling of their language. The difference between this ancient spelling and modern pronunciation produces many puzzling inconsistencies. In these outlines, I use a phonetic system to indicate roughly how Tibetan words are pronounced. Correct traditional spellings can be found in the glossary.

III. The next major series of events in Tibetan Buddhist history occurred in the eighth century, during the reign of King Thrisong Detsen.

A. Thrisong Detsen sponsored the construction of a monastery at Samye, the first Buddhist monastery in Tibet.

1. The construction of the monastery required the help of the Tantric saint Padmasambhava, also known as Guru Rinpoche ("Precious Teacher"). With his magic power, Padmasambhava subdued the demons that opposed the monastery's construction.
2. King Thrisong Detsen also enlisted the help of the Indian scholar named Shantarakshita to establish the curriculum in his new monastery.
3. Padmasambhava and Shantarakshita represent the two faces of Tibetan Buddhism: a reverence for the power of a Tantric practitioner and a reverence for the practice of Buddhist scholasticism.

B. Tibetan tradition also tells us that Thrisong Detsen sponsored a debate at Samye to determine the character of Tibetan Buddhism.
1. Representing the Chinese side was a meditation master named Mahayana who advocated a practice of sudden awakening.
2. Representing the Indian side was a disciple of Shantarakshita named Kamalashila who advocated a practice of gradual awakening.
3. According to Tibetan tradition, the king decided in favor of the Indian party and permanently oriented Tibet toward India.

C. The First Diffusion of Buddhism came to an end around the year 836, when a king named Langdarma attempted to suppress Buddhism. He was assassinated, and the line of Tibetan kings was broken.

IV. The "Later Diffusion" of the Dharma in Tibet took place during the 11th century.

A. Important teachers, such as Atisha (982–1054) and the Tantric saint Marpa (1012–96), reintroduced the tradition of monastic learning from eastern India.

B. From these tentative beginnings, and others like them, grew most of the schools that have dominated Tibetan Buddhism to the present day.
1. The Nyingma, or "Old," School traces its origin back to the First Diffusion of the Dharma, in the eighth century C.E.

2. The Kagyu, or "Teaching Lineage," School traces its origin to the Lama (guru) Marpa, whose disciple Milarepa (1040–1123) became one of Tibet's most beloved saints. The story of Milarepa's first meeting with Marpa gives a sense of the robust, down-to-earth quality of this tradition:

By the side of the road, a large, corpulent monk with sparkling eyes was plowing a field. As soon as I saw him, I felt inexpressible and inconceivable bliss. For a moment, his appearance stopped me in my tracks. Then I said: "Sir, I have been told that Marpa the translator, direct disciple of the glorious Naropa, lives in this place. Where is his house?"

For a long time he looked me up and down. Then he said: "Where are you from?"

I said: "I am a great sinner from upper Tsang. He is so famous that I have come to ask him for the true Dharma."

He said: "I will introduce you to Marpa, but now plow this field."

From the ground he pulled some beer that had been hidden under a hat, and he gave it to me. It was good beer, and it tasted great.

He said, "Plow hard," and he went away.

Mi la ras pa'i rnam thar (*Texte Tibetain de la vie de Milarepa*), ed. J. W. de Jong (Dordrecht: Mouton & Co., 1959), translated by Malcolm David Eckel.

3. The Sakya School emerged in the 11th century under the leadership of Drogmi (992–1074). Drogmi was the teacher of Konchog Gyeltsen who, in 1073, founded the Sakya Monastery that gave the school its name.

4. The Geluk, or "Virtuous Way," School (also known as the "Yellow Hats") emerged in the early 14th century under the leadership of the scholar Tsongkhapa. Tsongkhapa founded several major monasteries in central Tibet, including Ganden, his home monastery.

These have been some of the most influential religious institutions in the history of Tibet.

V. Tibetan Buddhism is personified for many people today by the figure of the Dalai Lama.

    A. The Dalai Lama received the Nobel Peace Prize in 1989 for his peaceful resistance to Chinese rule in Tibet. From exile in India, the Dalai Lama has traveled the world to champion the Tibetan cause and present Buddhist solutions to many of the problems that plague the modern world.

    B. The present Dalai Lama represents a line of incarnations that goes back to the 14th century.

        1. The title "Dalai Lama" was given to the third member of the lineage, Sonam Gyatso (1543–1589), by a Mongol leader named Altan Khan.

        2. The "Great Fifth" Dalai Lama (1617–1683) made the Dalai Lamas the spiritual, as well as the temporal or political, leaders of Tibet—bringing the ideal of the righteous king and the charismatic monk together in the same person.

        3. The first Dalai Lama to become enmeshed in international politics was the 13th (1876–1935).

        4. The weight of international responsibility has fallen most heavily, however, on Tenzin Gyatso, the 14th Dalai Lama.

    C. The 14th Dalai Lama functions as a bridge between the ancient cultural traditions of Tibet and the complex challenges that face many modern Buddhists at the turn of the 21st century.

Essential Reading:

Robinson and Johnson, *The Buddhist Religion*, ch. 11.

Dalai Lama, *Freedom in Exile*.

Supplementary Reading:

Strong, *The Experience of Buddhism*, ch. 7.

Lhalungpa, *The Life of Milarepa*.

Many of the Dalai Lama's speeches are available on Web sites, such as www.dalailama.com.

Questions to Consider:

1. Tibet shows again how important royal patronage has been to the establishment of Buddhism in new regions. Does the Tibetan case tell us anything more about the Buddhist alliance between monks and kings?

2. If you have an opportunity to read the public pronouncements of the Dalai Lama on the Internet or elsewhere, how do you think he has adapted Buddhist teaching for a modern Western audience?

Lecture Ten—Transcript
Buddhism in Tibet

If you had been alive in India sometime in the latter half of the first millennium of the Common Era, say, between the years 600 and the year 1200, it would have been a great time to be a Buddhist. In fact, it would have been a great time to be a Buddhist intellectual. That was the time when all of the wonderfully rich Mahayana traditions, the Mahayana philosophy, the Mahayana devotion, the Mahayana ritual that we've talked about in our earlier lectures, and also all of the complicated meditative and ritual practices of the Tantra had been absorbed in to the life of the Indian monasteries. These monasteries had large libraries and colorful rituals and an elaborate monastic curriculum ranging all the way from Buddhist philosophy and meditation to astronomy and medicine. They really were the great universities of their time.

Unfortunately, their cultural strength turned out, in the end, to be a major weakness when waves of raiders began to sweep down from Afghanistan across northern India. The monasteries were tempting targets for plunder and destruction. By the year 1200, after two centuries of pretty severe persecution, there wasn't much left of Buddhist monastic culture other than a handful of destitute, old monks. To trace the Mahayana tradition, now, we have to move beyond the Himalayas to Tibet, where Indian monastic culture has been preserved more faithfully and more richly than anywhere else in the Buddhist world.

The story begins in the seventh century in a movement that's known as the "First Diffusion" of the Dharma into Tibet. During the seventh century, a line of kings in central Tibet united the Tibetan tribes together and began to extend their military influence outside the Tibetan plateau. They sent military expeditions up into Central Asia. They even formed alliances with some people in China to attack the Chinese capitol. They began to come into contact with cultures and civilizations very different from the ones that they knew high on the Tibetan plateau. What they encountered, of course, as we know from our study, at least of South and Southeast Asia, was a series of lively Buddhist cultures in India, Nepal, Central Asia, and also in China.

According to Tibetan traditions, a king by the name of Songtsen Gampo, who lived approximately, the dates are a little bit unclear here, from about 609 to 649, invited one of his two Buddhist wives to help him introduce the cult of the Buddha into Tibet. I should say to you here, I think, now that I've mentioned my first Tibetan name, the name of the King of Songtsen Gampo, that the spelling of Tibetan words is particularly problematic. That won't be much of an issue for those of you who are listening on audiotape, but if you are watching this video and seeing the names being flashed on the screen, you'll realize that they are complex and sometimes difficult to pronounce. One of the reasons why Tibetan spelling is so problematic is that it was fixed about 1200 years ago. The pronunciation of Tibetan names has now evolved and diverged pretty substantially from the spelling. What you'll normally encounter, as in a course like this, would be something like an intuitive phonetic spelling of the name: Songtsen Gampo. I will list it or use it on the screen in a phonetic form. You can look in the glossary that accompanies this course to see the strict traditional spelling, which will be quite different from the phonetic spelling that I'll be using in speaking to you.

In any case, King Songtsen Gampo attempted to establish a cult of the Buddha in Central Tibet. His initial attempts to build a temple in the capitol city, Lhasa, failed. The carts that were carrying the Buddha image into Central Tibet, according to the traditions, sank into a swamp. They couldn't be moved to be able to construct this temple. The King wondered why he was running into this obstruction. In a dream he was told that the land of Tibet lay on the body of a demoness who had to be subdued before the Cult of the Buddha could be introduced into Tibet. He ordered a series of temples to be built around Tibet to pin down the knees and the elbows, the hips and the shoulders of this supine demoness who constituted the nation, the land of Tibet.

Finally, once she had been pinned down, he built a temple in Lhasa over her heart and installed this image of the Buddha in that temple. The temple is called the Jokhang. It's the central cathedral in Lhasa, and it is the most sacred site in Tibet. It represents, you'd have to say I think, the center of the mandala that's constituted by the land of Tibet with all of these monasteries pinning down the form of the demoness who constituted the land of Tibet.

In the Jokhang, this temple in Lhasa is an image called the Jobo Rinpoche, known traditionally as Songtsen Gampo's first Buddha image. The next major series of events associated with the first introduction of Buddhism to Tibet occurred in the eighth century during the reign of another Buddhist king Thrisong Detsen. Thrisong Detsen sponsored the construction of a monastery, the first monastery in Tibet at a place called Samye. The construction of the monastery required the help of a Tantric saint whose name was Padmasambhava, also know in Tibetan tradition as Guru Rinpoche, or "Precious Teacher."

You probably know the word "guru" from the study of Indian religion. It's a common word. It's used often in our culture. It means "teacher" in Sanskrit. The Tibetan version of the word guru is Lama. It refers to Tibetan teacher, as in the title of the Dalai Lama. Lamas are so important in Tibetan Buddhism that the tradition is sometimes actually referred to as Lama-ism as the tradition associated particularly with the Lamas, or the teachers.

In any case, Padmasambhava, or Guru Rinpoche used his magic power, according to the traditions that are told about this monastery, to subdue the demons that opposed the monastery's construction. King Thrisong Detsen also enlisted the help of an Indian scholar by the name of Shantarakshita, to establish the monastic curriculum in this new monastery. I think we can say, looking back retrospectively on this event, that Padmasambhava and Shantarakshita—these two figures associated with the founding of this first monastery—represent the two faces of Tibetan Buddhism: A great reverence for the power of a Tantric saint, a Tantric practitioner, and also a reverence for the practice of Buddhist scholasticism, the complex intellectual discipline of Buddhist philosophy represented by Shantarakshita.

Tibetan tradition also tells us that Thrisong Detsen sponsored a debate at Samye to determine the character of Tibetan Buddhism. There was a representative of the Chinese side. Chinese monks were also present in Tibet at this time. His name was simply Mahayana. He advocated the meditative practice of sudden awakening. Representing the Indian side, according to the traditions that we have about this debate, was the disciple of Shantarakshita, whose name was Kamalashila. He advocated a practice of gradual awakening. According to Tibetan tradition, the king decided in favor of the Indian party and permanently oriented the Tibetan tradition in the direction of India. It was from India that inspiration came in later centuries to form the distinctive traditions of Tibet.

The First Diffusion of Buddhism in Tibet came to an end around the year 836, when a king by the name of Langdarma attempted to suppress Buddhism. There had been parties in his court who had become jealous of the influence of Buddhist monks, and Langdarma was enlisted to suppress Buddhist influence in Central Tibet. He was assassinated, and the line of Tibetan kings was broken. Buddhism fell into a period that was really like the Dark Ages. Buddhism really disappeared from Central Tibet for a century or two.

The later diffusion of the Dharma in Tibet took place during the 11th century when Buddhism was re-introduced into Central Tibet by a series of important teachers like Atisha, an Indian scholar who lived from 982 to 1054, and also by the Tantric saint, Marpa, who was a Tibetan master who traveled to India, studied with a bunch of Indian saints, and then brought their tradition back to Tibet to form one of the major lineages of Tibetan Buddhism. It was out of these tentative beginnings in the 1000s, in the 11th century, that most of the schools that have dominated Tibetan Buddhism to the present day actually emerged.

Let me tell you about some of those schools so that you can get a sense of the denominational character of Tibetan Buddhism and a sense of some of its distinctive traditions. The first school to mention, because it's the oldest, is the Nyingma School. The name means simply "Old." "Nyingma"—"Old." It traces its origin back to the First Diffusion of the Dharma in the eighth century in the figure of Padmasambhava. You might well ask, if you're following this narrative, how they traced their lineage back to Padmasambhava. Were there texts, were there teachers, who still passed along the doctrine or the teaching of Padmasambhava, himself? The answer to that question is really no, at least not in any direct sense. The lineage was broken.

The Nyingma has a really remarkable teaching about the persistence of hidden texts in Tibet that were left behind by Padmasambhava and then rediscovered by teachers in some future time. Sometimes, in a physical sense, texts that were hidden in monasteries and then rediscovered two or three or four hundred years after the death of Padmasambhava, but sometimes texts that were implanted in the minds of his key disciples so that when they—through the process of death and rebirth came to be reborn in Tibet in subsequent centuries—they could go into states of deep meditation or have great visions or dreams and have these texts re-appear to them.

One of the most distinctive practices in the Nyingma tradition is a practice associated with what we call *termas*, or treasures, hidden texts that had been planted in the minds of the disciples of Padmasambhava to manifest themselves in some future time. You can see here, once again interestingly enough, how important scriptures are in passing on the authority of the Buddhist tradition. Obviously, Buddhists pay tremendous respect to meditative achievement. The meditative achievement often is validated only in the generation of some new text that is either scriptural in form or is based in some way on a scriptural transmission. All of you should search for memories right now and see whether you think there's some hidden text or message from Padmasambhava that has somehow been implanted in the stream of your consciousness waiting to manifest itself seemingly by accident at this moment.

In any case, the Nyingma tradition traces its origin back to Padmasambhava and has developed a very lively and very distinctive series of practices and traditions based on the recollections of that remarkable figure. It's lively and active in the Tibetan community today.

Another lineage that is lively and active and quite remarkable is the Kagyu, or Teaching School, that traces its origin back to the Lama Marpa, who I mentioned earlier lived in the 11th century. His disciple, Milarepa, became one of Tibet's most beloved saints. The story of Milarepa actually is one of the classic saints' biographies, I think, in the history of the religious traditions of the world. The biography in a nutshell is that he was a young man in a family where his father died. His relatives unjustly seized the family property. His mother became very resentful of this. She attempted to enlist Milarepa's help to wreak revenge on the relatives. She sent Milarepa, this young boy, out to study with a black magician so he could learn the arts of magic to seek revenge on the relatives and call down a hailstorm and various other natural events that killed members of the relatives' families.

He became so overwhelmed by feelings of guilt about what he had done that he went off to a series of teachers to try to achieve some kind of awakening that would relieve him of the burden of these sinful actions. He went to a few different teachers, none of whom really worked for him. Finally, he ended up meeting the Lama that he was destined to study with, Lama Marpa. Marpa put him through a series of intense, very painful trials: building a tower, tearing the tower down, building it up again, tearing it down, perhaps, with some understanding that he had to put Milarepa through a series of very harsh penances in some way to burn away the effect of his previous karma. In any case, Marpa eventually gave Milarepa the teaching that he needed and made it possible for him to go off and meditate on his own and achieve the kind of breakthrough that he was seeking. It's his humility and his persistence and also the wit and charm of some of his songs that have really made him one of the most beloved and characteristic of all Tibetan saints.

The episode in Milarepa's biography that intrigues me the most because of its simplicity—because it's so down to earth—is the story of Milarepa's first encounter with his teacher Marpa. Let me read you just a couple of lines of it. "Milarepa was off seeking Marpa. He knew he lived in a certain region. He didn't know what he looked like. He didn't know where the house was. He was walking down the road, and he came upon a figure plowing a field. By the side of the road, a large, corpulent monk with sparkling eyes was plowing a field. As soon as I saw him I felt inexpressible and inconceivable bliss." I wish I could say this about the feelings of students who walk into my classes. I'm not sure that it happens, at least all the time. "As soon as I saw him I felt inexpressible and inconceivable bliss. For a moment his appearance stopped me in my tracks. Then I said, 'Sir, I have been told that Marpa the translator, direct disciple of the glorious Naropa, lives in this place. Where is his house?'

"For a long time, he looked me up and down, then he said, 'Where are you from? What part of the county do you come from?' I said, 'I am a great sinner from the Upper Tsang. He is so famous, that I have come to ask him for the true Dharma.' He said, 'I will introduce you to Marpa, but now plow this field.' From the ground he pulled some beer that had been hidden under a hat, and he gave it to me. It was good beer, and it tasted great. He said, 'Plow hard,' and he went away."

Just this remarkable Tibetan combination between something that is down to earth—it's earthy, simple, direct, and also speaks of a powerful spiritual connection between a teacher and a student, out of which grew eventually the extraordinary career of this great saint, Milarepa. This tradition continues, of course, to the present day. It's lively, not just in some of the countries that border Tibet, in Bhutan and some of the other countries on the southern rim of the Himalayas, but also there are important communities associated with the Kagyu tradition in America today. The Naropa Institute, for example, in Boulder, Colorado, is associated with this lineage and teaches very much in the tradition of Marpa and Milarepa.

Another important school in Tibetan Buddhism is known as the Sakya School. It emerged in the 11th century under the leadership of a monk by the name of Drogmi, who lived 992–1074. Drogmi was the teacher of a man by the name of Konchog Gyeltsen who, in 1073, founded the Sakya Monastery that gave the school its name. The Sakya School was very important in the history of Tibetan Buddhism during the Second Diffusion of the Dharma. The early Sakya monks had very close relations with some of the Mongol princes. They helped, not only establish the influence of the Sakya School in Central Tibet, but to help cultivate Tibetan Buddhism amongst the Mongols. They continue, in various ways, to be influential among Tibetan refugees and in Tibetan communities, today.

The school that's the most well known, I suspect in America, is the school that's associated with the Dalai Lama. This is called the Geluk, or the "Virtuous Way," School. It's also known as the "School of the Yellow Hats." Perhaps you've seen photographs of Tibetan monks that have yellow hats that have fringe on them, and they come up and come over the top of the head to a point in the front. These are hats that are used particularly by Gelugpa monks when they engage in ritualized debate.

The Geluk School emerged in the early 14th century under the leadership of a scholar by the name of Tsongkhapa. Tsongkhapa founded several major monasteries in Central Tibet, including his own home monastery which is called Ganden. These have been some of the most influential religious institutions in the history of Tibet because they really became the home monasteries of the lineage of the Dalai Lamas. Actually, I had a very wonderful visit up to the monastery at Ganden just a few years ago, and, as often, learned what seemed to me to be some very important things about Tibetan Buddhism by simply being on the site that was associated with this great figure, Tsongkhapa.

At Ganden, people who come on pilgrimage to the monastery walk around the monastery. They do a circumambulation around the mountaintop where the monastery is located, and, as they go around it, the object of the pilgrimage is to try to discern the places in the rock where Tsongkhapa has laid his hands and miraculously placed his handprints. You have the experience on this kind of a pilgrimage of going with a group of Tibetan monks and Tibetan laypeople, laughingly feeling the rock, trying to see if you can discern the handprint of Tsongkhapa. The claim always is that if you have enough faith, you'll be able to see it. I can't claim to have had any miraculous visions, but I did enjoy the trip. It was wonderful to walk in the footsteps of such a great scholar, the Scholar Tsongkhapa.

Today, I think it would be true to say that Tibetan Buddhism is personified for most people by the figure of the Dalai Lama. The Dalai Lama received the Nobel Peace Prize in 1989 for his peaceful resistance to Chinese rule in Tibet. From exile in India, the Dalai Lama has traveled the world to champion the Tibetan cause and to present Buddhist solutions to many of the problems that plague the modern world, including issues of human rights and problems with the exploitation of the environment. The present Dalai Lama represents a line of incarnations that goes back to the 14th century. In fact, I think we should recognize and note in passing that one of the most distinctive aspects of Tibetan Buddhism is the idea that Lamas, great teachers, reincarnate themselves from one generation to the next to keep the lineage alive.

One of the big issues in Tibetan Buddhism when a Lama dies is how to find the reincarnation of the important master and bring the child back to the monastery to be trained to reassume the authority of the person who has just passed away. That happens often in Tibetan communities and has been a particular issue in the succession of authority in the lineage of the Dalai Lamas. The title "Dalai Lama" was given to the third member of the lineage, whose name was Sonam Gyatso, who lived in the 16th century in the 1500s. The title was given to him by a Mongol leader named Altan Khan. The word "*dalai*" is a Mongol word that means "ocean," and presumably refers to the Dalai Lama as an ocean of wisdom.

The lineage continued beyond Sonam Gyatso. A number of key figures are probably worth mentioning. The "Great Fifth" Dalai Lama lived in the 17th century, from 1617 to 1683. He's the one who built the great palace in Central Tibet that, I think, would be associated for many people with the image of the Dalai Lama. It's the so-called Potala Palace. It sits on a ridge just north of the center of Lhasa, like a great bird on top of a mountain ridge, one of the most beautiful and impressive Buddhist buildings in the world. He also is the one who made the Dalai Lamas the spiritual as well as the temporal, or political, leaders of Tibet.

The monks in Central Tibet had been involved, by that time, for a couple of centuries in political negotiations amongst themselves for political hegemony in ways that are not dissimilar to the political issues that we talked about in my last lecture about Southeast Asia. Mongol princes had some influence. There were some local Tibetan princes who played a role, and there also were some other important monastic organizations besides the Galugpas. It turned out just by accident, during this time, that the competing powers were quite weak. The "Great Fifth" Dalai Lama was a very strong and forceful leader, and he managed to seize power and make himself both a political leader of Tibet and also the religious leader, bringing together the ideal of the righteous king, or the *dhamma-raja* that we spoke about last time, and also the charismatic monk in a single person, the person of the Dalai Lama.

The first Dalai Lama to become enmeshed in international power politics was the 13th Dalai Lama, who got caught in the political negotiations between Russia in the north; China in the east; and British-controlled India, in the south. It was during his life that the British sent a major military expedition into Lhasa to establish some kind of influence over the Tibetan Regime. From about the year 1915 up until the end of the Second World War, the British had established a diplomatic presence in Tibet.

I think you'd have to say that the weight of international responsibility fell most heavily on Tenzin Gyatso, the 14th Dalai Lama who was born after the death of the 13th Dalai Lama, in 1935. As a young man, he had to try to respond to Chinese pressure, and eventually to the Chinese attack on Tibet. He was not able to do so successfully, at least, not able to preserve the independence of Tibet, and he had to flee Tibet to establish a residence in exile in northern India. He travels the world now to teach the values of Tibetan Buddhism, teach the values of Buddhism more generally around the world.

People often ask me when we talk about the Dalai Lama, how people were able to discover him. He's a remarkable person, actually. You would have to say he has occupied the responsibilities of that position with remarkable grace and energy. The answer to the question about his discovery begins with the figure who was appointed as the regent to act in the Dalai Lama's stead after the death of the 13th Dalai Lama. He went down to a lake in southern Tibet and had a vision of a village up in the north where the child was to be born. He sent a series of emissaries up to northern Tibet, carrying with them possessions that had belonged to the 13th Dalai Lama. When they found the boy who was the likely candidate in a little village that looked like the village that had been seen in the dream or in the vision at the lake in southern Tibet, they presented this child with the old possessions of the Dalai Lama mixed in with a whole series of other things. According to the story, with uncanny accuracy, he picked out precisely those things that had belonged to him in a previous life.

The representatives of the regent then had to negotiate with the Chinese to bring the boy to Lhasa and raise him and train him for the position of the Dalai Lama. He's been a truly remarkable person and one who is well worth observing and paying attention to as a spokesman, not just for the lively and engaging traditions of Tibet, but for Buddhism more generally. Well worth our attention I suspect, even as introductory students of this wonderful tradition.

Lecture Eleven
Buddhism in China

Scope:

Buddhism entered China in the second century of the Common Era, at a time when China was suffering from political turmoil and cultural decline. The Chinese people had become disillusioned with traditional Confucian values and saw Buddhism as a new way to solve enduring religious and cultural problems. To bridge the gap between India and China, the earliest Buddhist translators used Taoist vocabulary to express Buddhist ideas. Through a long process of interaction with Taoism, Confucianism, and Chinese popular religion, Buddhism took on a distinctively Chinese character, becoming more respectful of duties to the family and the ancestors, more pragmatic and this-worldly, and more consistent with traditional Chinese respect for harmony with nature. The combination of Indian and Chinese values is vividly displayed in the meditation tradition known as Ch'an, the precursor of Son Buddhism in Korea and Zen Buddhism in Japan.

Outline

I. By the time Buddhism entered Tibet, there had been Buddhists in China for more than 500 years. In this lecture, we will consider the process of transformation that took place as the first few generations of Chinese Buddhists struggled to understand the significance of this foreign tradition and adapt it to the distinctive needs of Chinese culture and Chinese people.

II. When the first Buddhist monks began to appear in the Chinese capital in the middle of the second century C.E., China was coming to the end of one of the most prosperous periods in its history.

    A. During the Han Dynasty (206 B.C.E–220 C.E.), China was culturally and politically stable.

        1. The prosperity of Han China was closely tied to an ideological synthesis known as Han Confucianism.

        2. Starting from the teaching of Confucius (c. 500 B.C.E.), scholars created a vision of heaven, earth, the family, and human society as a single, harmonious whole.

3. The key values were harmony, respect for elders, and a sense that society was bound together by the proper performance of ritual.

B. In the middle of the second century, the Han synthesis began to fall apart.

1. The emperor came under the influence of rival factions in the court and no longer had the power or the moral force to guarantee the legitimacy of the state.
2. As factions struggled for power, the peasants were increasingly alienated and oppressed.
3. Intellectuals looked for new ways to diagnose and respond to the moral malaise of the times.

C. China was ripe for the introduction of new ideas, even ideas as foreign as the teaching of the Buddha.

III. Buddhism had to go through a long process of adaptation before it could become a major part of Chinese civilization.

A. As Buddhist monks made their way into China and tried to communicate Buddhist ideas in a Chinese way, they faced difficult barriers.

1. Sanskrit and Chinese were radically different languages and expressed radically different systems of thought.
2. One of the key differences had to do with the family.
3. Chinese social values emphasized the family, while Buddhism stressed the rejection of the family as part of the path to awakening.

B. Buddhist monks adapted to these challenges in several ways.

1. Sanskrit and Chinese terms were matched with one another so that key Buddhist ideas were matched with ideas already familiar to Chinese audiences. For example, the word *dharma* was matched with the Chinese word *tao*.
2. Offensive concepts often were omitted, and aspects of the Indian tradition that were particularly congenial to Chinese tastes were emphasized, such as the image of the bodhisattva Vimalakirti, who maintained his loyalty to the family while pursuing the path of the Buddha.

C. One of the key components in the Chinese adaptation of Buddhism was a sense of kinship between Buddhism and the indigenous Chinese tradition of Taoism.

1. Taoism was comparable in antiquity to the tradition of Confucius.
2. In contrast to the active, public virtues of Confucianism, Taoism advocated a strategy of inactivity and contemplation.
3. The Taoist "Way," or *Tao*, was down to earth, natural, harmonious, and inexpressible in words.
4. We can see the kinship between Taoism and Buddhism by looking at a few passages in the *Tao-te Ching*, one of the fundamental texts of the Taoist tradition:

The Tao that can be told of is not the eternal Tao;
The name that can be named is not the eternal name.
The Nameless is the origin of Heaven and Earth;
The Named is the mother of all things.

The Tao is empty like a bowl.
It may be used but its capacity is never exhausted.
It is bottomless, perhaps the ancestor of things.
It blunts its sharpness,
It unties tangles,
It softens its light.
It becomes one with the dusty world.

Thirty spokes are united around the hub to make a wheel,
But it is on its non-being that the utility of the carriage depends.
Clay is molded to form a utensil,
But it is on its non-being that the utility of the utensil depends.
Doors and windows are cut out to make a room,
But it is on its non-being that the utility of the room depends.
Therefore turn being to advantage, and turn non-being into utility.

From Wing-tsit Chan, *A Sourcebook of Chinese Philosophy* (Princeton: Princeton University Press, 1969), ch. 7.

5. We can imagine how Buddhists, with their reverence for simplicity, renunciation, and emptiness would have been delighted to hear these words.
6. In the hard times that followed the fall of the Han Dynasty, Taoism offered an effective survival strategy for the beleaguered intelligentsia. It also offered a rich body of words and ideas to express Buddhism in a Chinese way.
7. While Taoism had a philosophical side, it was not as elaborate as the Indian analysis of, for example, the self.

D. Although the connection with Taoism offered Buddhists an important cultural opportunity, it also changed Buddhist values in important ways.

1. Buddhism became more pragmatic and down-to-earth.
2. Nature became an important concept in Chinese Buddhism as it never had been in India. The Tao is associated with the movements of nature and was often found by withdrawing into a natural environment.
3. Buddhism became much more amenable to the possibility of sudden enlightenment.

IV. During the T'ang Dynasty (618–907), these influences became clear when Buddhism became the dominant religious tradition in China.

A. The T'ang Dynasty saw the development of several important Buddhist schools, including the meditation school known in China as Ch'an and in Japan as Zen.

1. The Ch'an School is traced to the legendary Indian saint Bodhidharma (fl. 460–534).
2. According to tradition, Ch'an began to take on a Chinese character in the hands of Hung-jen (601–674) and, particularly, in the hands of his disciples Shen-hsiu (605?–706) and Hui-neng (638–713).
3. One version of the conflict between these two disciples is found in the Platform Sutra of the Sixth Patriarch.
4. Hui-neng advocated a position of sudden awakening, while Shen-hsiu advocated gradual awakening.

5. In response to a challenge from the master to write a short verse expressing his understanding of awakening, Shen-hsiu wrote:

The body is the tree of perfect wisdom
The mind is the stand of a bright mirror.
At all times diligently wipe it.
Do not allow it to become dusty.

6. Hui-neng replied:

Fundamentally perfect wisdom has no tree.
Nor has the bright mirror any stand.
Buddha-nature is forever clear and pure.
Where is there any dust?

From Wing-tsit Chan, *A Sourcebook of Chinese Philosophy* (Princeton: Princeton University Press, 1969), ch. 26.

7. The Ch'an tradition's distrust of words, its love of paradox, and its emphasis on direct, person-to-person transmission of insight had much in common with Taoism.

B. Mahayana devotional traditions also had great influence during the T'ang Dynasty.

1. For peasants and villagers, the promise of salvation in Amitabha's land held out hope for a future life. For the elite, it offered a type of contemplation that was very different from the austere practice of Ch'an, as in the words of Tao-ch'o (d. 645):

Suppose a man in an empty and distant place encounters a bandit who, drawing his sword, comes forcefully and directly to kill him. This man runs straight on, looking ahead to cross a river....

So also is the practitioner. When he is contemplating Amita [Amitabha] Buddha, he is like the man contemplating the crossing. The thought is continuous, no others being mingled with it.

From Wm. Theodore de Bary, ed., *Sources of Chinese Tradition* (New York: Columbia University Press, 1960), p. 385.

2. For many people, the cult of bodhisattvas, including Avalokiteshvara (Kuan-yin), promised not just rebirth in another world but direct assistance with the concerns of this life, such as the birth of a child or prosperity in the family.

C. Buddhist values had broad influence on Chinese literature and the arts.

1. The poet who is known simply as Cold Mountain wrote some of the Buddhist tradition's finest contemplative verses about nature. For example:

As for me, I delight in the everyday Way,
Among mist-wrapped vines and rocky caves.
Here in the wilderness I am completely free,
With my friends, the white clouds, idling forever.
There are roads, but they do not reach the world;
Since I am mindless, who can rouse my thoughts?
On a bed of stone I sit, alone in the night,
While the round moon climbs up Cold Mountain.

From Burton Watson, trans., *Cold Mountain: 100 Poems by the T'ang Poet Han-shan* (New York: Columbia University Press, 1970), p. 67.

2. Wang Wei gave poetic expression to a distinctively Chinese three-stage view of Emptiness:

Empty hills, no one in sight,
only the sound of someone talking;
late sunlight enters the deep wood,
shining over the green moss again.

From Burton Watson, *Chinese Lyricism: Shih Poetry from the Second to the Twelfth Century* (New York: Columbia University Press, 1971), p. 173.

V. The Buddhism of Vietnam is largely derived from China.

A. There is a lively tradition of Ch'an Buddhism in Vietnam (as in the work of the Vietnamese monk Thich Nhat Hanh).

B. Vietnamese Buddhists also share the Chinese reverence for powerful Buddhas and bodhisattvas, such as Amitabha and Avalokiteshvara.

Essential Reading:

Wright, *Buddhism in Chinese History*, chs. 1–5

Supplementary Reading:

Robinson and Johnson, *The Buddhist Religion*, ch. 8.

Strong, *The Experience of Buddhism*, Chinese selections in ch. 8.

Chan, *A Sourcebook of Chinese Philosophy*, ch. 7 ("The Natural Way of Lao Tzu"), ch. 19 ("Neo-Taoism"), ch. 21 ("Seng-chao's Doctrine of Reality"), chs. 24–26.

Watson, *Cold Mountain*.

Questions to Consider:

1. It is sometimes said that Buddhists do not seek converts for their tradition, yet Buddhism spread aggressively through the countries of Asia, even to countries as remote and as confident in their own cultures as China. Why did Buddhists feel such an impulse to spread their faith?

2. The relationship between Taoism and Buddhism in China raises major questions about cultural influence and religious change. Why were Buddhists and Taoists able to adopt each other's ways of looking at the world so readily? What does this tell us about the character of both traditions?

Lecture Eleven—Transcript
Buddhism in China

As we continue to survey the development of Buddhism in Asia, it's time finally, I think, to turn our attention to China. By the time Buddhism entered Tibet, there had been Buddhists in China for over 500 years. In this lecture, we'll consider the process of transformation that took place as the first few generations of Chinese Buddhists struggle to understand the significance of this foreign tradition and adapt it to the distinctive needs of Chinese culture and the Chinese people.

When the first Buddhist monks began to appear in the Chinese capital in the middle of the second century of the Common Era, that's pretty early, I think we can remind ourselves, in the history of Buddhism. You remember perhaps that the Mahayana tradition only began to emerge in Indian Buddhism right around the beginning of the Common Era. When Buddhist monks began to make their way into China in the middle of the second century of the Common Era, the Mahayana was just beginning to flourish in some form in the Indian tradition.

At this time, in the second century of the Common Era, China was coming to the end of one of the most prosperous eras in its history. During the Han Dynasty that lasted from 206 B.C.E. to 220 C.E., China was stable culturally and stable politically. The prosperity of Han China was closely tied to an ideological synthesis that we now refer to as Han Confucianism, a tradition that was derived from the teaching of the sage Confucius, who lived about 500 years or so B.C.E.

Starting from the teaching of Confucius, scholars had created a vision of heaven, earth, family, and human society—all existing together as a single harmonious whole. I am far from being a scholar of Confucianism, so I can't comment to you in any kind of authoritative way about this tradition. I don't think it's unfair to say that the key values for Confucian people, for scholars, and also for Confucian bureaucrats and for the common people who made up Confucian society in China—the key values were harmony, respect for elders, as we say, piety, respect for elders, and a sense that society was bound together by the proper performance of ritual. This particular Confucian concept I've always found difficult to speak to my students about in the classroom at Boston University because you know 17- and 18- and 19-year old students are not particularly respectful of precise performance of ritual behavior.

To get some sense of why ritual was significant for the Confucian tradition and why it might actually be considered a value that would tie society together, we often do a simple experiment of shaking hands and imagining ourselves in a social role where greeting somebody by shaking hands might actually convey some very important information to them about yourself and about your sense of respect for them. I ask everybody to stand up and find a neighbor and then imagine that they're going for a job interview or going to meet somebody important and simply hold their hand out and greet the other person and sense what the best way is to establish some sense of mutual respect and social connection with that other person. It's very easy to see in a practical setting how simple rituals like that can have profound social effect. You can convey an enormous amount of information to somebody about your sense of self and your sense of them simply by the way you reach out, grasp their hand, and establish that basic form of social contact.

The Confucian vision of society was really of a very large structure of social interaction tied together by rituals of that sort, not just the small rituals like shaking hands, but the much larger rituals that the emperor would perform from time-to-time to establish the connection between human beings and the cosmos, the rituals that are performed to tie a family together or a community together or whatever. All of these ritual actions bound the world of Chinese civilization together into a harmonious pattern.

This vision of the world was obviously very effective in stable and prosperous times, but as the Han Dynasty began to disintegrate, the system of Confucian values began to fall apart with the decline of the dynasty. People began to look around for other kinds of values that they could use to deal with the challenges of ordinary human life. In the middle of the second century, the Han synthesis did indeed begin to fall apart. The emperor came under the influence of rival factions in the court and no longer had the power or the moral authority to guarantee the legitimacy of the state. As factions struggled for power, the peasants were increasingly alienated and oppressed.

Intellectuals, the kind of people to whom Buddhist monks would normally begin to preach their new teaching, looked for new ways to diagnose and respond to the moral difficulties of the time. I think you'd have to say that China was really ripe, in this period at the end of the second century of the Common Era, for the introduction of new ideas, even ideas as foreign and as fundamentally strange as the teaching of the Buddha, imported through central Asia from India.

Buddhism, truth be told, had a long way to go before it could become a major part of Chinese civilization. As Buddhist monks made their way into China, coming across the Silk Road through Central Asia, they began to try to communicate Buddhist ideas in a Chinese way. They faced some barriers that I think are pretty easy for us to understand. Sanskrit and Chinese simply as languages were radically different. They expressed radically different systems of thought. The kind of philosophy that would be natural to articulate in a Sanskrit medium, the kind of philosophy that we've been talking about in at least some of our lectures in earlier segments of this course, simply doesn't translate well into the Chinese language and to Chinese patterns of thinking.

A key difference between Indian civilization, and particularly between Buddhism and Chinese social values, has to do with Chinese emphasis on the family. The family is really the center for many people in articulation and practice of Confucian values. In Buddhism, the major emphasis is really on rejection of the family. Just looking back at the story of the Buddha himself, the crucial moment in his early life came when he left behind his wife and his young child and joined a group of wandering monks in the forest. This would be a very strange idea to the Chinese.

The Buddhists had to overcome some barriers before they could begin to express Buddhism in a way that would be attractive in Chinese civilization. One of the strategies they used to make this adaptation was to match Sanskrit and Chinese terms, to find suitable terms in Chinese that could be used to translate Sanskrit words. They weren't always great translations, but at least they allowed people to make a certain kind of intuitive connection. For example, the word *dharma*, such an important word in traditional Buddhism, the word that we use to name the Buddha's teaching, was matched with the Chinese word "*tao*," that means simply "the way," so that "*dharma*" became "the way," like the way of Confucius, or the way, as we'll see in a few moments, of the Taoist tradition.

Often, Buddhist monks simply omitted offensive concepts. They left out aspects of the Indian tradition that were particularly uncongenial to Chinese tastes, such as the renunciation of the family. They emphasized images drawn from the Mahayana sutras that the Chinese might instinctively resonate with, like the image of the bodhisattva Vimalakirti, who was a great Buddhist sage, but also lived at home with his family and lived an active social life in the ordinary lay context. By some shrewd concept matching, and also by being rather selective about the things that they presented to the Chinese, they began to make some initial connections.

They were only able to dig more deeply into their contact with Chinese culture when they began to plumb the relationship with the indigenous Chinese religious tradition known as Taoism. They sense, I think quite rightly, that there was a particular kinship between Indian Buddhist values and the values of this great Chinese tradition. Taoism was comparable in antiquity to Confucianism. In contrast to the active public virtues of Confucianism, Taoism advocated a strategy of inactivity and contemplation. How wonderful. You can imagine how attractive this would have seemed to a Buddhist monk encountering Chinese civilization for the first time.

The Taoist "Way," or the *Tao*, was down to earth, it was natural. It had to do with a harmonious relationship with the movements of the natural world. It emphasized the value of harmony as the Confucian tradition did. The Taoist way was inexpressible in words, much like the Buddhist concept of nirvana or the Buddhist concept of Emptiness.

We can see the kinship between Taoism and Buddhism by looking at a few passages for the *Tao Te Ching*, one of the fundamental texts of the Taoist tradition. The very first verse emphasizes the inexpressibility of the Tao. The Tao that can be told of is not the eternal Tao. The name that can be named is not the eternal name. The nameless is the origin of heaven and earth. The named is the mother of all things. Remember Vimalakirti's silence, how they questioned Vimalakirti about the so-called Dharma door of non-duality. The most profound response to that question was Vimalakirti's refusal to say anything at all. How marvelous to put that story in juxtaposition with this opening chapter of the *Tao Te Ching*. The two seem to be working with language in very similar ways. It seems to suggest to us that we can make some more profound connections between these two traditions.

Another verse speaks about emptiness in a way that would be very congenial to Mahayana philosophers. The Tao is empty like a bowl. It may be used, but its capacity is never exhausted. It is bottomless. Perhaps it's the ancestor of things. It blunts its sharpness. It unties tangles. It softens its light. It becomes one with the dusty world. You remember how difficult it was for us to talk about emptiness here together. It's a very problematic concept, especially when it's expressed in abstract form. Here in the *Tao Te Ching*, in these Taoist scriptures, we have a very concrete, very down to earth image, of emptiness as an empty bowl out of which all things come. It can never be exhausted, a very rich poetic image of the positive dimension of the Emptiness concept, potentially in the Mahayana tradition.

Here's another vision of emptiness as a source of power and effectiveness and activity. Thirty spokes are united around the hub to make a wheel, but it's on its non-being that the utility of the carriage depends. It's on the empty space at the hub of the wheel that the effectiveness of the carriage revolves. Clay is molded to form a utensil, but it's on its non-being that the utility of the utensil depends. Doors and windows are cut out to make a room, but it's on its non-being that the utility of the room depends. Therefore, turn being to advantage and turn non-being into utility.

We've struggled often in our lectures in this course to try to get some sense of the positive resonance of the image of non-being, of no-self, of Emptiness in the Buddhist tradition. Here we're encountering a Chinese tradition that reveres images of negativity in the same way. Non-being here is a very positive way of viewing something like the source of potentiality, the place out of which utility arises in the flow of ordinary experience. We can imagine how Buddhists, with their reverence for simplicity, renunciation, and emptiness would have been delighted to hear these words.

In the hard times that followed the fall of the Han Dynasty, Taoism offered an effective survival strategy for the beleaguered intelligentsia. It also, not incidentally, offered a very rich body of words and ideas to express Buddhism in a Chinese way. It helped the Chinese intellectuals listen to Buddhist teaching with receptive ears.

While the connection with Taoism offered Buddhists an important cultural opportunity, I think we also have to acknowledge that it changed Buddhist values in important ways as well. Buddhism had to become more pragmatic and down to earth in order to exploit this connection with Taoism. Taoism certainly had a philosophical side, as Buddhism did, but it had nothing as elaborate as the Indian analysis, for example, of the five components of the personality, and certainly nothing as intense analytically as the philosophical exploration of the Emptiness doctrine in India. Buddhism had to find ways to express itself that were more down to earth, more pragmatic, more concerned with experience in this world. Nature became an important concept in Chinese Buddhism as it had never been in India because the Tao is associated with the movements of the natural world. It was often found in Chinese experience by withdrawing into a natural environment.

Buddhism had to become much more amenable to the possibility of a sudden experience of enlightenment. Chinese tradition wasn't particularly concerned, at least initially, with seeking some kind of salvation that was outside of this world. Salvation or transformation or awakening or whatever it was you were seeking came here, suddenly, in the experience of this world. All of these values were absorbed by the Buddhist tradition and transformed Mahayana Buddhism in significant ways. These influences became clear, finally, in Chinese history during the T'ang Dynasty, which lasted from the year 618 to 907, when Buddhism became the dominant religious tradition in China. The T'ang Dynasty saw the development of several important Buddhist schools, including the meditation school known in China as Ch'an and in Japan as Zen.

The Ch'an School is traced historically to a legendary Indian saint by the name of Bodhidharma, who flourished, according to the tradition, from around 460 to 534. It began to take on a distinctively Chinese character in the hands of a Ch'an master by the name of Hung-jen, and then finally in the hands of his disciples, Shen-hsiu and Hui-neng, who lived at the end of the seventh century and at the beginning of the eighth. One version of the conflict, if that's the right word, between these two disciples is found in the Platform Sutra of the Sixth Patriarch, a text that is associated with Hui-neng, who is known retrospectively as the Sixth Patriarch. Hui-neng, in this text, advocated a position of sudden awakening, while Shen-hsiu advocated gradual awakening.

Let me tell you what this means. Those terms may come to you simply like words scratched on a blackboard. It would be a good idea to have a story here to try to put some of this in context. Happily, the Ch'an tradition out of which these two figures come is rich in marvelous stories of experiences of sudden awakening. The story of Hui-neng goes something like this: He is an illiterate figure from the provinces who comes to the monastery to seek teaching about awakening. The master challenges him and says, "Who are you? Where do you come from?" He says, "I come from some provincial region. The master says, "We really can't teach a barbarian like you." Hui-neng says to the master, "There is no north or south in the Buddha nature. Why should there be north or south in the choosing of a disciple to hear the teaching?" The master receives him, allows him to become a student in the monastery, and then sends him out to do some menial labor.

In the meantime, he schedules a verse competition to decide who will receive the mantle of his authority in the next generation. Students are challenged to write a verse that expresses their understanding of awakening. Shen-hsiu, the lead monk in the monastery, the A-student you might say, writes a verse that goes like this: "The body is the tree of perfect wisdom. The mind is the stand of a bright mirror. At all times diligently wipe it. Do not allow it to become dusty." Classic statement about the diligent practice of meditation. It would lead you to some kind of awakening.

Hui-neng heard about this verse and dictated a response of his own. It goes like this: "Fundamentally, perfect wisdom has no tree, nor has the bright mirror any stand. Buddha nature is forever clear and pure. Where is there any dust?" Classic statement about emptiness. You remember when we were talking about emptiness just a couple of lectures ago, I said that if you take the doctrine of non-duality, or the understanding of emptiness as non-duality, literally there is no barrier between us at this moment and the Buddha. Here Hui-neng is making precisely that assertion. Fundamentally, perfect wisdom has no tree, nor has the bright mirror any stand, the mirror of the mind. Buddha nature is forever clear and pure. Where is there any dust? Why is there any need to engage in some kind of diligent practice to seek awakening, as if awakening were something different from the experience of the present moment?

This love of paradox and stress on sudden enlightenment has characterized the Ch'an tradition from that day to this. It has a remarkable distrust of words. It loves paradoxical expression. It emphasizes direct person-to-person transmission of insight, in much the same way that the Taoist tradition did in classical China.

The Ch'an school was not the only form of Mahayana Buddhism to develop in this period. There were other philosophical schools as well. There also were devotional traditions that were significant in the spread of Buddhism in China. For peasants and villagers, the promise of salvation in Amitabha's Pure Land held out hope for a happy future life. For the elite, it often offered a type of contemplation that was very different from the austere practice of Ch'an.

One place to see this is in the words of a Chinese Pure Land teacher by the name of Tao-ch'o. Suppose a man in an empty and distant place encounters a bandit who, drawing his sword, comes forcefully and directly to kill him. This man runs straight on and, looking ahead, crosses a river. So, also, does the practitioner. When he is contemplating Amita, or Amitabha Buddha, he is like the man contemplating the crossing. The thought is continuous, no others being mingled with it. This is a teaching here of single-minded intense focused contemplation on the figure of Amitabha Buddha and the possibility of rebirth in the Pure Land.

For many people, also the cult of celestial bodhisattvas—such as Avalokiteshvara, or as Avalokiteshvara is called in China, Kuan-yin, promised not just rebirth in another world, but direct assistance with the problems of this life, such as the birth of a child or prosperity in the family.

I think I mentioned to you when we were talking about celestial bodhisattvas and Buddhas a few lectures ago, that I made a visit not so long ago, a couple of years ago, to a pilgrimage site on an island off the coast of southern China that's sacred to the bodhisattva Avalokiteshvara, or Kuan-yin. It's remarkable to see how lively the cult of Kuan-yin is today in China. People come from all over China and from many parts of the overseas Chinese community to invoke the aid of Kuan-yin for prosperity in the family, and also do the other things that have to do with the practice of Buddhist pilgrimage, moving from shrine-to-shrine, carrying incense bags, where you get the incense bag stamped with an amulet that will in some way be used to ensure your passage into a good rebirth in the next life, and also visit a cave that's referred to as "the cave of tidal sound," where people traditionally have sought visions of the bodhisattva Kuan-yin.

The devotional traditions of the Mahayana that were so important to the spread of the Mahayana in India also played a tremendously significant role in the spread of Mahayana Buddhism in China.

Buddhist values also had broad influence during the T'ang Dynasty, and in later periods, on Chinese literature and the arts. One of my favorite Chinese Buddhist poets is a figure who is known simply as Cold Mountain, Han-shan. He wrote some of the Buddhist tradition's finest contemplative verses about nature. You got a sense in his verses of the transformation that's taken place in Buddhism as it begins to absorb some of the Taoist respect for the natural world. "As for me," he says, "I delight in the everyday way, among mist-wrapped vines and rocky caves. Here in the wilderness I am completely free, with my friends, the white clouds, idling forever. There are roads, but they do not reach the world. Since I am mindless, who can rouse my thoughts? On a bed of stone I sit, alone in the night, while the round moon climbs up Cold Mountain."

When we talk about this poem in my classes on Buddhism at Boston University, I often challenge students to sit down with a piece of paper and just jot down the elements of this poem that remind them of Indian Buddhism, and then jot down the elements that remind them of Chinese Taoism, and then try to identify the ways these elements have been fused in the mind of the poet to bring these two traditions together into a single aesthetic unity.

I think you could say from the Indian point of view, that we have here a classic image of the solitary wanderer, just like the solitary wandering sage of the Buddha as he made his way across the roads of northern India. There's an image of freedom. Nirvana, above all, for Indian Buddhists is an experience of freedom. This freedom is beyond the world. The world, I suppose, we could understand as a way of designating some sorrow, the realm of death and rebirth. The moon that's referred to in the last line is a classic old Indian symbol for the coolness, for the quiet, of the Buddha. There was a tradition in India actually that the rays of the moon cooled you if you slept outside at night in the same way that the rays of the sun warm you during the daytime. The coolness of the Buddha's contemplation is associated with the moon. All of these are Indian resonances in this poem.

Chinese resonances, where would we look for those? The idea that the poet has become unified with nature, settled into a natural setting in order to experience his awakening and become a sage, the idea of the everyday way, the *Tao*, that is associated with everyday common experiences, that down-to-earth pragmatic image of the way, comes very strongly from the Taoist tradition. When he says, "I am mindless," he's referring to a Taoist line in which the sage is viewed as having no mind of his own, but simply absorbing himself in the natural world. All of these are Chinese resonances.

You can see how the two traditions also have been so closely merged that it's very difficult in the end to pull them apart. I think we can say that, although it took many centuries, the Buddhist tradition went through a remarkable period of transfer process of transformation in China, in which it shaped itself from a tradition that was radically different from anything that the Chinese would ever find acceptable to a tradition that had become very deeply merged with the ancient wisdom of Chinese culture, and in the process transformed the Buddhist tradition itself profoundly.

Lecture Twelve
Buddhism in Japan

Scope:

Buddhism entered Japan in the sixth century of the Common Era. In the early years, in the reign of Prince Shotoku (574–622) and the Nara period (710–84), Buddhism was tied closely to the welfare of the nation. When the imperial capital was moved to Kyoto in the ninth century, new Buddhist schools emerged and changed the face of Japanese Buddhism. The Shingon School, founded by Kukai (774–835), brought the colorful symbols and rituals of Tantra to Japan. The Tendai School, founded by Saicho (767–822), introduced the synthesis of the Chinese T'ien-t'ai School and served as the foundation for three great Buddhist schools that have dominated Buddhist life in Japan until the present day: the Pure Land Buddhism associated with the reformers Honen (1133–1212) and Shinran (1173–1262), the prophetic Buddhism of Nichiren (1222–1282), and the Zen tradition associated with such Zen masters as Dogen (1200–1253).

Outline

I. Buddhism entered Japan as early as the year 535 from Korea, at a time when the Japanese were suffering from some of the same difficulties the Chinese had experienced a few centuries earlier, during the fall of the Han Dynasty.

    A. In their search for an effective model, the Japanese turned to China and found a combination of Confucian and Buddhist values.

    B. Although the Japanese borrowed Chinese traditions, they also had different orientations and different needs.

        1. Buddhist values had to be placed in some kind of relationship with the indigenous Japanese tradition that we know today as Shinto, or "the Way of the Gods."

        2. Shinto is sometimes called the indigenous nature and spirit worship of Japan.

        3. The most important deity in Shinto tradition is the sun goddess Amaterasu. The rising sun is the symbol of Japan, and the power of the sun goddess is understood as being present in the lineage of the emperors.

C. The presence of Shinto posed a distinctive challenge to Buddhism in Japan.
   1. Were the Shinto and Buddhist deities rivals, or were they manifestations of the same power?
   2. When Buddhism first entered Japan, some Japanese perceived Buddhism as a threat, but the two traditions eventually were perceived as complementary, and the *kami* and the Buddhas could be worshipped together.

II. Prince Shotoku (573–621) and the Seventeen-Article Constitution.

A. One of the most important figures in the early history of Japanese Buddhism was Prince Shotoku. As the regent during the reign of his aunt, Shotoku led Japan through a process of political reorganization.
   1. As he changed the procedures of the court to conform to Chinese models, most of Shotoku's reforms grew out of the Confucian values then popular in China.
   2. But Shotoku also was a convinced and devout Buddhist. He felt that Buddhism could also be used to unify the nation and promote the welfare of the Japanese people.

B. Prince Shotoku expressed his Confucian and Buddhist values in a manifesto called the Seventeen-Article Constitution.
   1. The first article shows the influence of the Confucian concept of a harmonious society:

   Harmony is to be valued, and avoidance of wanton opposition is to be honored. All men are influenced by partisanship, and there are few who are intelligent. Hence there are some who disobey their lords and fathers, or who maintain feuds with the neighboring villages. But when those above are harmonious and those below are friendly, and there is concord in the discussion of business, right views of things spontaneously gain acceptance. Then what is there which cannot be accomplished?

2. The second article shows the influence of Buddhism:

> Sincerely reverence the three treasures. The three treasures, viz. Buddha, the Law, and the Monastic orders, are the final refuge of the four generated beings, and are the supreme objects of faith in all countries. Few men are utterly bad. They may be taught to follow it. But if they do not betake to the three treasures, wherewithal shall their crookedness be made straight?

> From Wm. Theodore de Bary, ed., *Sources of Japanese Tradition* (New York: Columbia University Press, 1958), p. 50.

III. During the Nara period (710–784, named after the city that served as the imperial capital), less than a century after the death of Shotoku, Buddhism effectively became a state religion.

    A. Emperor Shomu (r. 724–49) sponsored a series of building projects that gave special prominence to Buddhism as an instrument of national policy.

        1. He constructed Todai-ji (the "Great Eastern Temple") as a symbol of the relationship between Buddhism and the Japanese state.

        2. The temple is said to be the largest wooden building in the world. It houses a colossal bronze statue of the Buddha, known as Dainichi ("Great Illumination"). This is the Japanese version of Vairochana, the Buddha of the Sun.

        3. According to tradition, the emperor sent messengers to the shrine of the Sun Goddess Amaterasu in Ise to seek her permission to erect a statue of Vairochana. The message that came back suggested that the Sun Buddha and the Sun Goddess were identical.

    B. At the end of the Nara period, the capital was moved to Kyoto, and Japan entered the Heian period (794–1185), a time of peace, prosperity, and courtly sophistication.

IV. The Heian period produced two important Buddhist schools.

    A. Kukai or Kobo Daishi (774–835) founded the Shingon ("True Word") School.

1. Kukai traveled to China to find an authentic form of Buddhist practice.
2. In the Chinese capital, he encountered Chen-yen, a Chinese version of the Mantrayana, or "Vehicle of Powerful Words." The word *Shingon*, which is the name of his school, is the Japanese form of the Chinese translation of Mantrayana.
3. The elaborate, colorful rituals of Shingon had immense appeal in the Heian court.

B. Saicho or Dengyo Daishi (762–822) founded the Tendai School.
1. Saicho stressed the importance of the Lotus Sutra and used the teaching of "one vehicle" as a unifying principle, with political, as well as religious, implications.
2. The significance of this concept is evident in his "Vow of Uninterrupted Study of the Lotus Sutra;"

The Disciple of the Buddha and student of the One Vehicle this day respectfully affirms before the Three Treasures that the saintly Emperor, on behalf of Japan and as a manifestation of his unconditional compassion, established the Lotus Sect and had the Lotus Sutra, its commentary, and the essays on Concentration and Insight copied and bound—together with hundreds of other volumes—and installed them in seven great temples. Constantly did he promote the Single and Only Vehicle, and he united all the people so that they might ride together in the ox-cart of the Mahayana to the ultimate destination, enlightenment.

From Wm. Theodore de Bary, ed., *Sources of Japanese Tradition* (New York: Columbia University Press, 1958), pp. 128–129.

V. The Kamakura period (1192–1333) saw the foundation of three new schools that changed the face of Japanese Buddhism.
A. The turbulence of the Kamakura period brought a feeling of pessimism to Buddhist life, but it also brought a new sense of opportunity.

1. Buddhist thinkers returned to the ancient Buddhist idea of a degenerate age (*mappo*, the degenerate age of the Dharma), when it was no longer possible for people to hope for salvation in a traditional way.
2. This sense of crisis gave a new urgency to their account of Buddhist practice.

B. Honen (1133–1212) and Shinran (1173–1262)—two Pure Land reformers—responded to this sense of crisis by preaching a radical reliance on the grace of Amitabha Buddha.

1. Honen believed that it was no longer possible to rely on one's own efforts to achieve salvation. The only way to be saved was simply to trust in the grace of Amida Buddha.
2. Honen's teaching is made clear in his "One-Page Testament," delivered to his disciples two days before he died:

The method of final salvation that I have propounded is neither a sort of meditation, such as has been practiced by many scholars in China and Japan, nor is it a repetition of the Buddha's name by those who have studied and understood the deep meaning of it. It is nothing but the mere repetition of the "Namu Amida Butsu," without a doubt of his mercy, whereby one may be born into the Land of Perfect Bliss. The mere repetition with firm faith includes all the practical details, such as the three-fold preparation of mind and the four practical rules. If I, as an individual, had any doctrine more profound than this, I should miss the mercy of the two honorable ones, Amida and Shaka [the historical Buddha and Shakyamuni] and be left out of the vow of Amida Buddha. Those who believe this, though they clearly understand all the teachings Shaka taught throughout his whole life, should behave themselves like simple-minded folk, who know not a single letter, or like ignorant monks or nuns whose faith is implicitly simple. Thus, without pedantic airs, they should fervently practice the repetition of the name of Amida, and that alone.

From Wm. Theodore de Bary, ed., *Sources of Japanese Tradition* (New York: Columbia University Press, 1958), pp. 208–209.

3. Shinran (1173–1262) adopted Honen's teaching and pushed it to a radical extreme. He expressed his faith in Amida in the following way:

> If even a good man can be reborn in the Pure Land, how much more so a wicked man!

> People generally think, however, that if even a wicked man can be reborn in the Pure Land, how much more so a good man! This latter view may at first sight seem reasonable, but it is not in accord with the purpose of the Original Vow, with faith in the Power of Another. The reason for this is that he, who relying on his own power, undertakes to perform meritorious deeds, has no intention of relying on the Power of Another and is not the object of the Original Vow of Amida. Should he, however, abandon his reliance on his own power and put his trust in the Power of Another, he can be reborn in the True Land of Recompense.

From Wm. Theodore de Bary, ed., *Sources of Japanese Tradition* (New York: Columbia University Press, 1958), p. 217.

C. Another key Kamakura reformer was Nichiren (1222–1281), one of the few people who can appropriately be called a Buddhist "prophet."

1. Nichiren felt that the Lotus Sutra was the key to the Buddha's teaching, and he preached that Japan could be saved only by reliance on the Lotus Sutra. This reliance was expressed by the phrase "Namu Myoho Renge Kyo" ("Homage to the Lotus Sutra").

2. The force of Nichiren's teaching is evident in his own words:

> When they hear me say that the Lotus Sutra is the only source of salvation for the Japanese people, the people will say that it is a curse; yet those who propagate the Lotus of Truth are indeed the parents of all men living in

Japan…. I, Nichiren, am the master and lord of the sovereign, as well as of the Buddhists of other schools. Notwithstanding this, the rulers and the people treat us maliciously. How should the sun and the moon bless them by giving light? Why should the earth not refuse to let them abide upon it? …Therefore, also, the Mongols are coming to chastise them. Even if all the soldiers from the five parts of India were called together, and the mountain of the Iron Wheel were fortified, how could they succeed in repelling the invasion? It is decreed that all the inhabitants of Japan shall suffer from the invaders. Whether this comes to pass or not will prove whether or not Nichiren is the propagator of the Lotus of Truth.

From Wm. Theodore de Bary, ed., *Sources of Japanese Tradition* (New York: Columbia University Press, 1958), p. 225.

D. The last Kamakura movement to be mentioned is the Japanese version of Ch'an Buddhism in China, the movement that is known in Japan as Zen.

   1. Zen took shape as a separate sect during the Kamakura period, under the influence of two forceful personalities: Eisai (1141–1215) and Dogen (1200–1253).

   2. Eisai developed the tradition known as Rinzai Zen, which uses the discipline of *koan* practice to achieve an experience of sudden awakening. A *koan* is a puzzle that is meant to stop the mind in its tracks, such as: "Does a dog have Buddha-nature?" or "What is the sound of one hand clapping?"

   3. Dogen thought that koan practice put too much stress on achieving awakening, as if it were different from ordinary experience. To correct this misunderstanding, he emphasized the practice of *zazen*, or "sitting meditation," as an end in itself.

   4. He also criticized the idea of a "degenerate age," arguing that all moments are equally reflective of Emptiness. A classic expression of this doctrine is found in his statement on "Being-Time:"

Know that in this way there are myriads of forms and hundreds of grasses throughout the entire earth, and yet each grass and each form itself is the entire earth. The study of this is the beginning of practice.

When you are at this place, there is just one grass, there is just one form; there is understanding of form and there is no-understanding of form; there is understanding of grass and no-understanding of grass. Since there is nothing but just this moment, the being-time is all the time there is. Grass-being, form-being are both time.

Each moment is all being, is the entire world. Reflect now whether any being or any world is left out of the present moment."

From Kazuo Tanahashi, ed., *Moon in a Dewdrop: Writings of Zen Master Dogen* (New York: North Point Press, 1985), p. 77.

5. Like other Zen masters, Dogen concentrates on the experience of the moment. If reality exists anywhere, it is in the infinitesimal moment of the present. If someone wants to be awakened, he or she has to find that awakening in the present moment of experience.

6. One of Dogen's most powerful statements about Zen is the Genjo Koan or "Actualizing the Fundamental Point:"

To study the Buddha way is to study the self. To study the self is to forget the self. To forget the self is be actualized by myriad things. When actualized by myriad things, your body and mind as well as the bodies and minds of others drop away. No trace of realization remains, and this no-trace continues endlessly....

Enlightenment is like the moon reflected on the water. The moon does not get wet, nor is the water broken. Although its light is wide and great, the moon is reflected even in a puddle an inch wide. The whole moon and the entire sky are reflected in dewdrops on the grass, or even in one drop of water.

From Kazuo Tanahashi, ed., *Moon in a Dewdrop: Writings of Zen Master Dogen* (New York: North Point Press, 1985), pp. 70–71.

VI. As we look back over the development of Buddhism from its origin in India to the varieties of Buddhism we experience in East Asia, we can see that Buddhism has changed so much that it often is difficult to see what makes it "Buddhist."

    A. Buddhist teaching has evolved from the simple formulas of the Four Noble Truths to include traditions of devotion to celestial Buddhas and bodhisattvas that would have been quite foreign to the early tradition, to say nothing of the immense philosophical complexities of Emptiness.

    B. The Buddhist community has grown from a simple community of monks and nuns and laypeople to include complex social and political movements that draw Buddhism into the center of a struggle for political power and national identity.

    C. Is there anything that has not changed?

    D. Perhaps it is simply the serene image of the Buddha himself, who remains an island of calm throughout the turbulent history of tradition that bears his name.

Essential Reading:

Robinson and Johnson, *The Buddhist Religion*, ch. 10.

Earhart, *Japanese Religion*, ch. 10.

Supplementary Reading:

Strong, *The Experience of Buddhism*, Japanese selections in ch. 8.

Earhart, *Japanese Religion*, chs. 1–9.

deBary, *Sources of Japanese Tradition*, chs. 10–11.

Suzuki, *Zen and Japanese Culture*.

Questions to Consider:

1. The introduction of Japanese Buddhism challenges us to think again about continuity and change. What new themes emerged in the formation of the Japanese tradition?

2. Honen, Shinran, and Nichiren were radical reformers. In what sense do you think they were still working out the original impulse that motivated the career of Siddhartha Gautama, the historical Buddha?

3. Do you think any of them went too far in their reinterpretation of Buddhism?

Lecture Twelve—Transcript
Buddhism in Japan

In our last lecture, we discussed the development of some of the key traditions in Chinese Buddhism. We want to finish our survey of Buddhism in Asia by taking a brief look at the Buddhism of Japan.

Buddhism entered Japan as early as the year 535 from Korea, at a time when the Japanese were suffering from some of the same difficulties that the Chinese had experienced a few centuries earlier during the fall of the Han Dynasty. In their search for an effective religious and political model to deal with some of these challenges, the Japanese turned to China and found there, as you might well imagine, a combination of Confucian and Buddhist values. While the Japanese borrowed these Chinese traditions, I think we also have to say that they had rather different religious orientations, and, as a result, some rather different and distinctive religious needs.

Buddhist values in Japan had to be placed in some kind of relationship with the indigenous Japanese religious tradition that we now know as Shinto, or "the Way of the Gods." Shinto is sometimes called the indigenous nature and spirit worship of Japan. The most important of these deities, the deities who were worshipped in the Shinto tradition, is known in Japanese by the name of *kami*. The most important of these deities is the sun goddess Amaterasu. The rising sun, as you know, is a symbol of the Japanese nation. The power of the sun goddess is understood as being present, and has been understood traditionally in Japan this way, as being present in the lineage of the Japanese emperors.

The presence of Shinto posed a distinctive challenge to Buddhism in Japan. People had to ask, were the Shinto and Buddhist deities to be understood as rivals? Were they the manifestations of a single power? When Buddhism first entered Japan, some Japanese perceived Buddhism as a threat. The two traditions eventually were perceived as complementary, as fitting together in a kind of harmonious way, so that the kami and the Buddhas could be worshipped together.

One of the most important figures in the early history of Japanese Buddhism was Prince Shotoku, who lived from 573 to 621. As the regent during the reign of his aunt, Shotoku led Japan through a process of political reorganization in which Confucian and Buddhist values became, as it were, the charter for the Japanese state. As he changed the procedures of the Japanese court to conform to Chinese models, most of Shotoku's reforms grew out of Confucian values that then were popular in China. Shotoku also was a convinced and devout Buddhist. He felt that Buddhism could also be used to unify the nation and promote the welfare of the Japanese people.

Prince Shotoku expressed his Confucianism and Buddhism in a manifesto called the Seventeen-Article Constitution. I won't read to you the Confucian articles of the constitution, but let me simply read to you the ones that express Buddhist values, to show you how explicit and how forthright he was in appropriating Buddhism as a matter of national policy. "Sincerely reverence the three treasures," he says. "The three treasures, namely, the Buddha, the Dharma, and the Monastic orders, are the final refuge of the four generated beings, and are the supreme objects of faith in all countries. Few men are utterly bad. They may be taught to follow it, but if they do not betake themselves to these three treasures, wherewithal shall their crookedness be made straight?"

I particularly like that last phrase. I'm not sure if that really faithfully represents the Japanese, but it's a wonderful English representation of what is very solemn political prose.

During the next period in Japanese history, the Nara period, which lasted from 710 to 784, and which is named after the city that served as the imperial capital during that period, less than a century after the death of Shotoku, Buddhism effectively became a state religion for Japan. Emperor Shomu sponsored a series of building projects that gave special prominence to Buddhism as an instrument of national policy. He constructed the "Great Eastern Temple," the Todai-ji, as a symbol of the relationship between Buddhism and the Japanese state. This temple is said to be the largest wooden building in the world and houses a colossal statue of the Buddha that's known in Japanese as Dainichi, the "Great Illumination." This is the Japanese version of the Buddha Vairochana, the Buddha of the Sun, who is associated with one of the great mandalas of Tantric tradition in India.

According to Japanese tradition, the emperor sent messengers to the shrine of Amaterasu to seek her permission to erect a statue of Vairochana. The message that came back suggested that the Sun Buddha and the Sun Goddess were identical, which is a good example of that mapping of Buddhist deities onto the indigenous deities of Japan in a way that permits Buddhism to borrow authority from—and also reinforce—the authority of the Shinto tradition that was present in Japanese life before the coming of Buddhism.

At the end of the Nara period, the capital was moved just a few miles away to the city of Kyoto, and Japan entered the Heian period, lasting from the end of the eighth century to the end of the 12th century. In the Heian period, Japan experienced a period of peace, prosperity, and of great courtly sophistication. It was a time in which the literary and courtly arts flowered to an extraordinary degree. The Heian period produced two important Buddhist schools that have continued to affect the history of Japanese Buddhism until the present day. Kukai or Kobo Daishi was a Buddhist master who founded the Shingon School. The word *Shingon* is translated as "True Word," and it represents the Chinese version of the old Indian name Mantrayana, which is used to name the Tantric tradition in India.

Kukai traveled to China in the hopes of finding an authentic form of Buddhist practice. In the Chinese capital he encountered Chen-yen, the Chinese version of the Mantrayana. The word *Shingon* is a translation of this Chinese word. The elaborate and colorful rituals of Shingon, based on the elaborate and powerful rituals of the Tantric tradition in India, had immense influence in the courtly circles of Heian society.

Another important figure in this period was the master Saicho or Dengyo Daishi, who founded a school known as Tendai. Saicho stressed the importance of the Lotus Sutra and used the teaching of one vehicle from the Lotus Sutra as a unifying principle with political as well as religious implications. You may remember this teaching from our first discussion of Mahayana Buddhism several lectures ago. The Lotus Sutra was the sutra that told the story of the father who attempted to lure the children out of the burning house by promising them multiple vehicles. Then when they got out, he offered them the single vehicle. There was some discussion about what this meant.

Here, in the figure of Saicho, the Japanese tradition makes use of this old teaching, not merely as a way of speaking about the significance of the Mahayana, but as a way of providing a unifying image for Japanese political life. If there is one vehicle, then there should be one nation. Around that one vehicle the nation should gather in order to focus its forces on a common purpose. Saicho expressed this in a text called the "Vow of Uninterrupted Study of the Lotus Sutra." "The Disciple of the Buddha and student of the one vehicle this day respectfully affirms before the three treasures that the saintly emperor, on behalf of Japan and as a manifestation of his unconditional compassion, established the Lotus Sect, and had the Lotus Sutra, its commentary, and the essays associated with it, copied and bound, together with hundreds of other volumes, and installed in seven great temples."

The Heian period was important historically for the development of all subsequent Japanese Buddhism. The period that concerns us the most in our survey of Japanese Buddhism is not really the Heian period as much as it is the period that followed, a period known as the Kamakura period, when the capital shifted to the city of Kamakura. The Kamakura period lasted from 1192 to the year 1333, and represented in Japanese history a time of great political turmoil. If the Heian period was a time of peace and prosperity, the Kamakura period was a time of threat, of danger, of imminent disaster, as feudal warlords fought with each other for control in the Japanese countryside.

The mood in the Buddhist tradition changed in a remarkable way. It was a time of great pessimism, when people really began to doubt whether it was possible to achieve salvation in the traditional ways that had been taught in Buddhist schools during the Heian period, or, for that matter, in Buddhist schools in China and in India. Strangely enough, out of this feeling of pessimism came an extraordinary recommitment to the basic teachings of some forms of Buddhist practice. It represents, in our study of Japanese tradition, in some ways, the mainspring of some of the most creative and powerful religious movements, not just in Japanese history, but in the history of the Buddhist tradition more generally.

During this period, Buddhist thinkers returned to an ancient Buddhist idea that we have not discussed previously in our study of this tradition, but one that was rather deeply rooted in India. It's the idea of a degenerate age. The word in Japanese is *mappo*. It's used to refer in India and elsewhere in Asia to a time in which Buddhism has declined to such a degree that you can no longer effectively practice some of the basic teachings of the faith, and you have to find some other more powerful way, as it were, to achieve the kind of salvation that was offered by the traditional teaching.

Responding to this idea of the degenerate age was a number of important figures. Two of the ones that I find most intriguing are Pure Land reformers, one by the name of Honen, who lived from 1133 to 1212, and another by the name of Shinran. Both of these reformers responded to the sense of crisis in the Kamakura period by preaching a radical reliance on the grace of Amitabha Buddha. Honen believed that it was no longer possible to rely on one's own efforts to achieve salvation. The only way to be saved was simply to trust in the grace of this great Buddha. Here you can put emphasis on the word "simply" because it was simple trust that was called for. Anything more complicated or sophisticated than that would simply get in the way of Amitabha's salvation.

Let me read a few lines of Honen to give you a flavor of his teaching. "The method of final salvation that I have propounded is neither a sort of meditation such as has been practiced by many scholars in China and Japan, nor is it a repetition of the Buddha's name by those who've studied and understood the deep meaning of it. It's nothing but the mere repetition of 'Namu Amida Butsu.'" This is the Japanese version of that old Indian chant that we talked about a few lectures ago, "namoh amitabaya buddhaya," homage to Amitabha Buddha. "It is nothing but the mere repetition of 'Namu Amida Butsu,' without a doubt of his mercy, whereby one may be born into the Land of Perfect Bliss. If I, as an individual, had any doctrine more profound than this, I should miss the mercy of the two honorable ones, Amida and Shaka [the historical Buddha and Shakyamuni] and be left out of the vow of Amida Buddha. Those who believe this, though they clearly understand all the teachings that Shaka taught throughout his whole life, should behave themselves like simple-minded folk who know not a single letter, or like ignorant monks or nuns whose faith is implicitly simple. Thus, without pedantic airs, they should fervently practice the repetition of the name of Amida, and that alone."

It's an extraordinary teaching. It's direct, powerful, and focused. I think it takes that tradition of devotion that we've studied elsewhere in the Mahayana to a level of intensity that we simply have not seen before. Shinran adopted Honen's teaching and pushed it to a radical extreme. He's a remarkably powerful religious thinker in that respect. He expressed his faith in Amida in the following way. If even a good man can be reborn in the Pure Land, how much more so a wicked man! People generally think, however, that if even a wicked man can be reborn in the Pure Land, how much more so a good man! This latter view may at first sight seem reasonable, but it's not in accord with the purpose of the Original Vow, with faith in the Power of Another. The reason for this is that he who, relying on his own power, undertakes to perform meritorious deeds, and has no intention of relying on the Power of Another and, thus, is not the object of the Original Vow of Amida."

Honen and Shinran brought a new intensity and focus to the tradition of Mahayana devotion, provoked in part by this immense religious crisis that seemed to afflict the minds and people during the Kamakura period in Japan.

Another great Kamakura reformer whose teaching has echoed to the present day is Nichiren, a person whom we can, I think, quite justifiably refer to as a Buddhist prophet. He preached his teaching with a tremendous challenging intensity, willing to criticize even the figure of the emperor himself. Again, I'll read just a few words of Nichiren so that you can get the feeling of the intensity of his teaching. "When they hear me say that the Lotus Sutra is the only source of salvation, the people will say that I am making a curse. Yet those who propagate the Lotus of Truth are indeed the parents of all men living in Japan. I, Nichiren, am the master and lord of the sovereign, higher even than the emperor, as well as the Buddhists of other schools. Notwithstanding this, the rulers and the people treat us maliciously. How should the sun and moon bless them by giving light? Why should the earth not refuse to let them abide upon it? ... Therefore, also, the Mongols are coming to chastise them."

I almost want to shake my finger at you as if I were threatening you the way Nichiren seems to be threatening the people of Japan. "Therefore also, the Mongols are coming to chastise them. Even if all the soldiers from the five parts of India were called together, and the mountain of the Iron Wheel were fortified, how could they succeed in repelling this horrible invasion? It is decreed that all the inhabitants of Japan shall suffer from these invaders, and whether this comes to pass or not will prove whether or not Nichiren is the propagator of the Lotus of Truth." Strong prophetic teaching, very different from anything that we've heard previously in Buddhism, but growing in a remarkable way out of the teaching of the Lotus Sutra, a very basic and important Mahayana text, somehow interacting in a strange chemical reaction with the religious mood of the Kamakura period in Japan.

The last Kamakura movement I want to mention is the Japanese version of Ch'an Buddhism, the meditation tradition of China. This movement is known in Japan, of course, as Zen. Zen took shape as a separate sect of Japanese Buddhism during the Kamakura period, under the influence of two forceful personalities. I wonder sometimes if there were any personalities that were not forceful during this time. One was the Zen master Eisai, who lived at the end of the 12th century, and Dogen, who lived in the middle of the 13th century.

Eisai developed the tradition that is known as Rinzai Zen, which uses the discipline of *koan* practice to achieve an experience of sudden awakening. We're well aware of the tradition of sudden awakening from the practice of Ch'an in China. A *koan* is a puzzle that's meant to stop the mind in its tracks. Questions like, "Does a dog have Buddha-nature?" is a common, very basic Zen koan, or, "What is the sound of one hand clapping?" That's another koan. The answers to these koans can't be wrapped out conceptually. You can't say, "Oh, great master, I think I have figured this out. I think I understand that does a dog have Buddha-nature can be understood in terms of the four different arguments in favor of Emptiness as borrowed from the Indian tradition." This is not the case. We're not talking here about an intellectual expression of the understanding of Emptiness, but something that's experiential and has to be worked out in a direct encounter with the teacher who poses the koan to you as a challenge to your own religious understanding.

Dogen, in contrast to Eisai, thought that koan practice put too much stress on the experience of awakening *per se*, and treated it as if it were different from ordinary experience. To correct this misunderstanding, Dogen emphasized the practice of what is known in Japanese as *zazen*, or "sitting meditation," simply as an end in itself, just to sit in meditation. He also criticized the idea of the "degenerate age" that was so prominent in the thinking of people like Honen and Nichiren. He argued that all moments of time are equally reflective of the experience of Emptiness.

A classic expression of this doctrine is found in Dogen's statement on "Being-Time." I'd like to read a piece of it to you because I think it really is once again one of the classic pieces of Buddhist rhetoric, and one of the finest expressions of Emptiness in the Japanese tradition. "Know that in this way there are myriads of forms and hundreds of grasses throughout the entire earth, and yet each grass and each form itself is the entire earth. The study of this is the beginning of practice. When you are at this place, there is just one grass. There is just one form. There is understanding of form, and there is no understanding of form. There is understanding of grass, and there is no understanding of grass."

If this seems puzzling, remember the way we talked about Emptiness as involving both the denial of something and the assertion of something. This balance in Mahayana rhetoric is really crucial to the application of Emptiness to a particular experience in a particular moment. "There is understanding of grass, and there is no understanding of grass. Since there is nothing but just this moment, the Being-Time is all the time there is—grass being, form being, are both time. Each moment is all being, is the entire world. Reflect now whether any being or any world is left out of the present moment."

You can see how this is a strong re-appropriation of the basic teaching of Emptiness, but also is an extraordinarily powerful rhetorical response to the challenge of this idea in the Kamakura period, that this time we live in is a horrible time, and we can't practice the Dharma conceivably in the way that would have been practiced by the Buddha during the Buddha's own lifetime. Dogen says, "What is the difference between this moment and any other moment? This moment contains within it by implication all time and all space."

Zen masters sometimes speak about meditation in ways that metaphorically are intended to bring you to a concentration simply on the experience of the moment. I've seen a teacher once hold up a stick and balance it on his finger and say, "The past is gone and won't come back. The future is not here yet. It's not something that we can yet experience. If reality exists anywhere, it is in this tiny infinitesimal moment of the present. If we want to be awakened, if that's what we want, we have to find that awakening in a concentration on this present moment of experience." This, to me, is a powerful expression of the doctrine of Emptiness and is expressed,

I think, very beautifully in the work of the Zen master Dogen and in the tradition that flows from his example.

There's a lot more that can be said of course about Japanese Buddhism, but we'll have to leave that for another course and for another day. Let's just take a few moments together, as our course now comes to a close, to remind ourselves of where we have been and how much we've accomplished in these 12 short lectures.

It's been a long journey since we first encountered the figure of the Buddha, walking those winding lanes in northern India with a few of his chosen disciples. We've seen that the story of the Buddha himself has gone through some extraordinary transformations, transformations that we never even would have imagined when we first began to tell the story of that Indian sage. We've heard about celestial Buddhas and bodhisattvas, who have created Pure Lands in the heavens where they can transport their believers who chant their names with faith. We've encountered the figures of wrathful Buddhas who trample on their enemies in an expression of deepest rage. We've encountered a figure of the Buddha as the union of male and female. We've also come to see (as images of the Buddha) all those wise figures in Tibet, China, and Japan, who have functioned as Buddhas in some way for their own disciples and their own students. Finally, as Dogen makes clear to us, we've seen that we can think of ourselves as Buddhas if we can simply take the doctrine of Emptiness seriously and focus on it in the experience of a single moment.

The Buddhist teaching has also evolved for us, from the simple expression of the Four Noble Truths to include traditions of devotion to celestial Buddhas and bodhisattvas that would have been quite foreign to the early tradition, to say nothing of the immense philosophical complexities of Emptiness. All of those things involved significant transformations of the doctrinal structure of Buddhist teaching.

We have also seen that our view of the Buddhist community has grown, from a simple group of monks and nuns and laypeople, to include complex social and political forces that draw Buddhism into the center of the struggle for political power and national identity. I think you'd have to say that Buddhism has changed so much in our hands and our experience that it's been hard for us many times to see what makes it Buddhist. There's probably no better illustration of the old Buddhist doctrine of Impermanence than the development of Buddhism itself.

As we conclude, let's ask ourselves, through all these changes, is there anything we can hold onto that's distinctively Buddhist? When I'm asked this question, I go back to that serene contemplative image of the Buddha himself, the image that we first visualized for ourselves when we began to place ourselves inside the Buddhist tradition. This is a figure who remains calm, quiet, and fearless in the face of tumultuous change. I hope that I've been able to convey some of the spirit of this figure to you during the course of these lectures. I hope that he will stay with you as you study the rest of the great religious traditions of the world.

Timeline

Before the Common Era (B.C.E)

1500–1000 .... The earliest hymns of the Veda

1000–500 .... The classical Upanishads

486 .... Death of the Buddha Siddhartha Gautama

c. 486.. First Buddhist Council

c. 386?...................................... Second Buddhist Council

269–238 .... Reign of King Asoka in India; introduction of Buddhism to Sri Lanka (Ceylon)

206 .... Beginning of the Han Dynasty in China

Common Era (C.E.)

First century .... Emergence of the Mahayana in India

c. 100.. Kushan Empire: Mathura and Gandhara styles of Buddhist art

Second century........................... Introduction of Buddhism to China; Madhyamaka School developed by Nagarjuna in India

220 .... End of the Han Dynasty in China

Fourth century........................... Yogachara School developed by Asanga and Vasubandhu in India

Fourth–sixth centuries................ Gupta Dynasty in India

Sixth century .... Emergence of Tantra in India

460–534 .... Bodhidharma, founder of the Ch'an School in China

531–597 .... Chih-i, founder of T'ien-t'ai School in China

1133–1212	Honen, founder of a separate Pure Land School in Japan
1141–1215	Eisai, founder of the Rinzai School of Zen in Japan
1173–1262	Shinran, founder of the True Pure Land School in Japan
1192–1333	Kamakura period in Japan
c. 1200	Destruction of Buddhism in India
1200–1253	Dogen, founder of the Soto School of Japanese Zen
1222–1281	Nichiren, founder of the Nichiren School in Japan
1357	Birth of Tsongkhapa, founder of the Geluk School in Tibet
1391	Birth of Gendun Drubpa, later recognized as the first Dalai Lama
1617–1683	The "Great Fifth" Dalai Lama
1644–1694	Matsuo Basho, Zen poet in Japan
1844	Eugene Burnouf's *L'introduction a l'histoire du buddhisme indien* published in Paris
1851–1868	Reign of King Mongkut (Rama IV) in Thailand
1880	Madame Blavatsky and Colonel Olcott convert to Buddhism in Ceylon
1893	World Parliament of Religions in Chicago
1935	Birth of Tenzin Gyatso, the 14th Dalai Lama
1951	Chinese occupation of Tibet
1989	Nobel Peace Prize presented to the Dalai Lama

Glossary

Amida: the Japanese name for Amitabha Buddha.

Amitabha ("Infinite Light"): the Buddha who is the focus of devotion in Pure Land Buddhism.

Aniconic image: represents the Buddha by symbols, by places associated with his life, or by his absence.

Arhant **ideal**: the pursuit of nirvana for one's own sake, in contrast to the bodhisattva ideal, in which the bodhisattva postpones nirvana to help others achieve the same goal.

Avalokiteshvara ("Lord Who Looks Down"): the celestial bodhisattva of compassion, known in China as Kuan-yin and in Tibet as Chenrezig.

Bodhicitta: the "mind of awakening," cultivated by a bodhisattva through a combination of wisdom and compassion.

bodhisattva: a future Buddha or "Buddha-to-be" who postpones nirvana in order to help others achieve nirvana.

Bon: the indigenous religious tradition in Tibet.

Buddhist Churches of America: the American branch of the Jodo Shinshu or True Pure Land sect of Japanese Buddhism.

Celestial Buddhas and *bodhisattvas*: Buddhas or bodhisattvas who have achieved extraordinary powers. These powers make it possible for them to reside in the heavens (hence the name "celestial") and to function as the Buddhist equivalents of Hindu gods.

Chakravartin: a "turner of the wheel" who becomes either a great king and turns the wheel of conquest or a religious teacher and turns the wheel of religious teaching.

Ch'an: the meditation school of Chinese Buddhism, precursor of Zen.

Ching-t'u ("Pure Land") School: a school of Chinese Buddhism related to the Pure Land tradition in Japan.

Confucianism: a Chinese philosophical system that stresses values of political and social responsibility. It is traced to the philosopher Confucius (551–479 B.C.E.).

Degenerate Age of the *Dharma* (*mappo*): the view that conditions in the world have declined to such an extent that traditional means of Buddhist perfection are impossible; a key idea in several schools of Japanese Buddhism during the Kamakura period.

***Dharma* (Pali *Dhamma*)**: the Buddha's teaching.

***Dharmaraja* (Pali *Dhammaraja*)**: a "righteous king" who protects and promulgates the Dharma.

Emptiness: the absence of identity in things, a fundamental teaching of Mahayana Buddhism.

Gandhara style: a style of Buddhist art that shows the influence of Greek craftsmen in the Hellenistic kingdoms in Afghanistan (c. 100 C.E.).

Geluk (dGe-lugs): one of the four major schools of Tibetan Buddhism, the school of the Dalai Lamas.

Gupta style: a style of Indian art associated with the Gupta Dynasty in north India (fourth to sixth centuries).

Han Confucianism: the Confucianism that was practiced during the Han Dynasty (206 B.C.E.–220 C.E.) in China.

Hinayana: "Lesser Vehicle," a term used in Mahayana literature to describe the teaching that preceded the Mahayana.

Hsi-lai Temple: a major Chinese Buddhist temple in Los Angeles.

Hua-yen ("Flower Garland") School: a school of Chinese Buddhist philosophy founded by Fa-tsang (643–712).

***Jataka* tales**: stories about the previous lives of the Buddha.

Jodo Shinshu: the True Pure Land sect founded by Shinran (1173–1262) in Japan.

Kagyu (bKa'-rgyud): one of the four major schools of Tibetan Buddhism.

Kami: an indigenous deity in Japan.

Karma: a Sanskrit word that means "action." Good actions bring a good rebirth, and bad actions bring a bad rebirth.

Kuan-yin: the Chinese name of Avalokiteshvara, the celestial bodhisattva of compassion.

Lama (bla-ma): a teacher in the Tibetan tradition.

Lotus sutra: an Indian Mahayana sutra that played a major role in the development of Chinese and Japanese Buddhism.

Madhyamaka: the "Middle Way" School of Mahayana philosophy, developed in India in the second or third century C.E. by the philosopher Nagarjuna.

Mahasamghika: the "Great Community," a sectarian movement that is thought to be the forerunner of the Mahayana.

Mahayana: the "Great Vehicle," a reform movement that appeared in the Buddhist community in India around the beginning of the Common Era. Eventually, the Mahayana dominated the Buddhism of Tibet, China, Japan, Korea, and Vietnam.

Maitreya: a bodhisattva who is venerated throughout the Buddhist world as the Buddha of the future.

Mandala: a sacred circle used in Tantric Buddhist ritual.

Mañjushri ("Charming Splendor"): the celestial bodhisattva of wisdom and the patron deity of scholars in Mahayana Buddhism.

Mantra: a sacred phrase whose syllables are believed to have power in their own right.

Mantrayana: the "Mantra Vehicle," a common term for Tantric Buddhism.

Mathura style: a style of Buddhist art associated with the region of Mathura in the Ganges Basin (c. 100 C.E.).

Meditation (*dhyani*) Buddhas: the five Buddhas who are associated with the five major points in a mandala.

Mt. Hiei: the home of the Tendai School in Japan.

Nembutsu: the phrase "*Namu Amida Butsu*" ("Homage to Amida Buddha"), used in Japanese Pure Land Buddhism to invoke the compassion of Amida (or Amitabha) Buddha.

Nirvana: cessation of suffering, the goal of Buddhist life.

Non-duality: a way of speaking about the doctrine of Emptiness in Mahayana Buddhism.

Nyingma (rNying-ma): one of the four major schools of Tibetan Buddhism, founded by Padmasambhava.

Om manipadme hum: a mantra used to invoke the power of the celestial bodhisattva Avalokiteshvara.

Pali: a language that is derived from Sanskrit and used in the scriptures of the Theravåda tradition in Southeast Asia.

Pali canon: the collection of Buddhist scriptures used by the Theravåda tradition.

Potala Palace: the palace of the Dalai Lamas in Tibet.

Prajna **(Pali *pañña*)**: wisdom, a crucial component of the path that leads to nirvana.

Pure Land: a celestial paradise thought to be the home of Amitabha Buddha in the Mahayana tradition.

Renunciant: someone who has renounced the ordinary duties and responsibilities of Indian society to escape from the cycle of reincarnation.

Rinzai School: a school of Japanese Zen, founded by Eisai (1141–1215).

Sakya (Sa-skya): one of the four major schools of Tibetan Buddhism.

Samadhi: mental concentration.

Samgha: the Buddhist community.

Samsara: the cycle of reincarnation.

Samye (bsam-yas): first Tibetan monastery and site of a famous debate that led to the acceptance of Indian Buddhism in Tibet.

Sanskrit: the language of ancient India.

Shingon ("True Word") School: a school of Japanese Buddhism founded by Kukai or Kobo Daishi (774–835).

Shinto: "the Way of the Gods" as opposed to "the Way of the Buddha" in Japan.

Sila: moral precepts. Traditionally, laypeople observe five precepts: no killing, no stealing, no lying, no abuse of sex, and no drinking of intoxicants.

Soto School: a school of Japanese Zen founded by Dogen (1200–1253).

Sthaviravada: the "Doctrine of the Elders," a sectarian movement that was the forerunner of Theravåda Buddhism.

Stupa: a reliquary mound originally used to contain the relics of the Buddha.

Sutra: a Buddhist scriptural text.

Tantra: the term originally means the warp in a piece of cloth, used to refer to a variety of Buddhism that appeared in India in the sixth century C.E.

Taoism: a Chinese religious and philosophical tradition that stresses the value of harmony with nature.

Tendai School: a school of Japanese Buddhism founded by Saicho or Dengyo Daishi (762–822).

Theravåda: the "Doctrine of the Elders," the only surviving example of the 18 *nikayas*, or "schools," of traditional Buddhism. The Theravåda is now the dominant form of Buddhism in Southeast Asia.

Three Baskets (*tripitaka*): the three sections of the Buddhist scriptures.

Three Jewels: the Buddha, Dharma, and Samgha, also known as the three refuges.

Tibetan Book of the Dead: a manual for ritual and meditation to guide the consciousness of someone who has recently died through the afterlife.

T'ien-t'ai ("Heavenly Terrace") School: a school of Chinese Buddhist philosophy founded by Chih-i (531–597).

Todai-ji: the Great Eastern Temple in Nara, Japan.

Tulku **(sprul-sku)**: the Tibetan word *tulku* was used traditionally to refer to the "manifestation" body of a Buddha. Here, it refers to a saint or other religious leader who is recognized as being reborn in a new form.

Upanishad: the portion of the Veda that contained the most extensive speculation about the nature of reality and the doctrine of reincarnation.

Vairocana ("Radiant") Buddha: one of the key Buddhas in Tantric Buddhism; played a particularly important role in the adaptation of Buddhism to Japan.

Vajrayana: "Diamond Vehicle," a common term for Tantric Buddhism.

Veda: the most ancient and authoritative scriptures of the Hindu tradition.

Vedanta: another name for the Upanishads, the "end of the Veda."

World Parliament of Religions: a meeting held in Chicago in 1893 that introduced many important Asian religious leaders to the West.

Wrathful Buddha: an image of the Buddha in destructive form, common in Tantric ritual and art.

Yab-yum: an image of a Buddha as the union of male and female, common in Tantric ritual and art.

Yogachara: the "Yoga Practice" School of Mahayana philosophy, founded in the fourth century by Asanga, with help from his brother Vasubandhu.

Zen: the meditation school of Japanese Buddhism.

Biographical Notes

Asoka: an Indian king (reigned 269–238 B.C.E.) who converted to Buddhism and became the prototype of a "righteous king" (*dhammaraja*).

Atisha (982–1054): an Indian scholar who played an important role in the Later Diffusion of the Dharma in Tibet.

Aung San Suu Kyi: the leader of a democratic protest movement in Burma and recipient of the 1991 Nobel Peace Prize.

Basho, Matsuo (1644–1694): a well-known Zen poet in Japan.

Blavatsky, Madame Helena Petrova: co-founder of the American Theosophical Society with Colonel Henry Steele Olcott in 1875, an early convert to Buddhism.

Bodhidharma (fl. 460–534): an Indian saint who is said to be the founder of the Ch'an School in China.

Chih-i (538–597): founder of the T'ien-t'ai School in China.

Cold Mountain: a Chinese Buddhist poet who was active during the T'ang Dynasty.

Confucius (551–479 B.C.E.): a Chinese philosopher who was the founder of the Confucian tradition.

Dalai Lama: the spiritual and temporal leader of Tibet, thought by Tibetans to be the manifestation of the bodhisattva Chenrezig or Avalokiteshvara. Tenzin Gyatso, the current Dalai Lama, is the 14th holder of this lineage.

Dharmapala, Anagarika (b. 1864): a Theravāda Buddhist from Ceylon who helped introduce Theravāda Buddhism to North America at the World Parliament of Religions in Chicago in 1893.

Dogen (1200–1253): founder of the Soto School of Zen.

Drogmi (992–1074): founder of the Sakya School in Tibet.

Eisai (1141–1215): founder of the Rinzai School of Zen.

Fa-tsang (643–712): founder of the Hua-yen ("Flower Garland") School of Chinese Buddhist philosophy.

Great Fifth Dalai Lama (1617–1683): the Dalai Lama who solidified the political power of the Geluk School in Tibet, builder of the Potala Palace in Lhasa.

Guru Rinpoche: another name for Padmasambhava.

Honen (1133–1212): a Pure Land reformer during the Kamakura period in Japan.

Hsuan-tsang (596–664): a well-known Chinese pilgrim and philosopher who visited India in the early part of the seventh century and brought Yogachara philosophy back to China.

Hui-neng (638–713): a disciple of Hung-jen and sixth patriarch of a particular lineage of Ch'an Buddhism in China.

Hung-Jen (601–674): the fifth patriarch of the Ch'an tradition in China.

Konchog Gyelpo (dKon-mchog rGyal-po): founded the Sakya Monastery in Tibet in 1073.

Kukai or **Kobo Daishi** (774–835): founder of the Shingon ("True Word") School in Japan.

Kuya (903–972): "the Saint of the Streets," an early advocate of Pure Land Buddhism in Japan.

Mahadeva: a monk whose scandalous behavior is said to have provoked the Second Buddhist Council.

Mahaprajapati: the Buddha's great aunt, ordained as the first Buddhist nun.

Maitreya: the Buddha to come after Shakyamuni.

Manjushri: the celestial bodhisattva of wisdom.

Marpa (1012–1096): founder of the Kagyu, or "Teaching Lineage," School in Tibet.

Milarepa (1040–1123): one of Tibet's most beloved saints.

Mongkut, King of Thailand (r. 1851–1868), also known as King Rama IV: served as a monk for more than 25 years before becoming king. As king, he instituted a major reform movement in the Thai Samgha.

Nagarjuna (second or third century C.E.): founder of the Madhyamaka School of Buddhist philosophy in India.

Nichiren (1222–1281): Buddhist reformer during the Kamakura period in Japan.

Olcott, Colonel Henry Steele: co-founder of the Theosophical Society with Madame Helena Petrova Blavatsky in 1875 and an early convert to Buddhism.

Padmasambhava (eighth century): a Tantric saint who played an important role in the introduction of Buddhism to Tibet during the First Diffusion of the Dharma; considered the founder of the Nyingma School in Tibet.

Saicho or Dengyo Daishi (762–822): founder of the Tendai School in Japan.

Shakyamuni: Siddhartha Gautama, the Buddha of this historical era.

Shantarakshita (eighth century): an Indian scholar who participated in the founding of the first Tibetan monastery.

Shinran (1173–1262): a Pure Land reformer during the Kamakura period in Japan.

Emperor Shomu (r. 724–749): the emperor who built the Great Eastern Temple in Nara and promoted Buddhism as state policy during the Nara period (710–784).

Prince Shotoku (574–622): Japanese prince who was instrumental in the adoption of Buddhism as a form of national policy.

Shunryu Suzuki (1905?-1971): established the San Francisco Zen Center and trained a number of important disciples, including Richard Baker Roshi.

Siddhartha Gautama: the name of the historical Buddha.

Songtsen Gampo (Srong-brtsan-sgam-po): king of Tibet from 627 to 649, credited with the introduction of Buddhism to Tibet.

Soyen Shaku: a Rinzai Zen master from Japan who brought Daisetz Teitaro Suzuki to North America after the World Parliament of Religions in Chicago in 1893.

Suzuki, Daisetz Teitaro: an influential early spokesman for Zen Buddhism in North America.

Thrisong Detsen (Khri-srong-lde-brtsan): king of Tibet from 754 to 797, founded the first Tibetan Buddhist monastery and presided over a debate that led to the acceptance of Indian Buddhism in Tibet.

Tsongkhapa (1357–1419): founder of the Geluk, or "Virtuous Way," School (also known as the "Yellow Hats") in Tibet.

Trungpa Rinpoche, Chogyam: a modern leader of Tibetan Buddhism, founder of the Naropa Institute in Boulder, Colorado.

Wang Wei: a Chinese Buddhist poet who was active during the T'ang Dynasty.

Wangyal, Geshe: founder of a Gelukpa meditation center in Washington, New Jersey.

Bibliography

Aung San Suu Kyi. *Freedom from Fear and Other Writings*. London: Penguin Books, 1991. The collected speeches of the 1991 recipient of the Nobel Peace Prize.

Basho , Matsuo. *The Narrow Road to the Deep North and Other Travel Sketches*. London: Penguin Books, 1966. A graceful translation and thorough analysis of the work of Japan's most respected Zen poet.

Berthier, Francois. *Reading Zen in the Rocks: The Japanese Dry Landscape Garden*. Chicago: University of Chicago Press, 2000. A fascinating and original study of Japanese contemplative gardens.

Brauen, Martin. *Mandala: Sacred Circle in Tibetan Buddhism*. Boston: Shambhala, 1997. A lively and informative account of the symbolism and ritual practices associated with the mandala. The book recently has gone out of print, but it is widely available in libraries and used book services.

Brown, W. Norman. *Man in the Universe: Some Continuities in Indian Thought*. Berkeley: University of California Press, 1970. Still the most concise and accessible introduction to the religious problematic of Indian thought. Unfortunately, this book is out of print, but it is widely available in libraries and used book services.

Chan, Wing-tsit. *A Sourcebook of Chinese Philosophy*. Princeton: Princeton University Press, 1969. A useful survey of the schools of Chinese philosophy with accurate, readable translations and informative introductions.

Ch'en, Kenneth. *Buddhism in China: A Historical Survey*. Princeton: Princeton University Press, 1964. A useful survey of the history of Buddhism in China.

Conze, Edward. *Buddhist Scriptures*. London: Penguin Books, 1959. A superb collection of Buddhist scriptural sources, strongest on the Indian tradition.

———. *The Large Sutra on Perfect Wisdom*. Berkeley: University of California Press, 1975. Translation of one of the Mahayana tradition's most influential sutras on the perfection of wisdom and Emptiness.

Craven, Roy C. *Indian Art: A Concise History*. Revised edition. London: Thames and Hudson, 1997. A compact and accurate summary of the history of Indian art.

Dalai Lama. *Freedom in Exile: The Autobiography of the Dalai Lama*. New York: HarperCollins, 1990. The most recent autobiographical statement by the current Dalai Lama.

deBary, Wm. Theodore, ed. *Sources of Chinese Tradition*. New York: Columbia University Press, 1960. An authoritative compendium of primary sources in translation covering the full range of Chinese history.

————, ed. *Sources of Japanese Tradition*. New York: Columbia University Press, 1958. Another authoritative compendium covering the sources of Japanese history.

Earhart, H. Byron. *Japanese Religion: Unity and Diversity*. Belmont, CA: Wadsworth, 1982. A useful introduction to the history of Japanese religion.

Eckel, Malcolm David. *To See the Buddha: A Philosopher's Quest for the Meaning of Emptiness*. Princeton: Princeton University Press, 1994. A study of the relationship between Indian Buddhist philosophy and the tradition of Mahayana devotion.

Faure, Bernard. *The Rhetoric of Immediacy: A Cultural Critique of Chan/Zen Buddhism*. Princeton: Princeton University Press, 1991. A critical study of the prevailing interpretative myths in the study of Zen Buddhism.

Fields, Rick. *How the Swans Came to the Lake: A Narrative History of Buddhism in America*. Boulder, CO: Shambhala, 1981. A graceful and inclusive survey of the introduction of Buddhism to North America, including commentary on early European contacts with Buddhism.

Hanh, Thich Nhat. *The Miracle of Mindfulness: A Manual on Meditation*. Boston: Beacon Press, 1987. A brief and eloquent account of Buddhist meditation by one of the most well known contemporary Vietnamese masters.

Huntington, Susan L. *The Art of Ancient India: Buddhist, Hindu, Jain*. New York: Weatherhill, 1985. A detailed and authoritative survey of the tradition of Indian art by the doyenne of Indian art in America.

Kalupahana, David J. *Buddhist Philosophy: A Historical Analysis*. Honolulu: University of Hawaii Press, 1976. A useful introduction to the diversity of Buddhist philosophy in the Indian tradition.

Lhalungpa, Lobsang P. *The Life of Milarepa*. Boulder, CO: Shambhala, 1984. A vivid and appealing translation of the biography of one of Tibet's most beloved saints.

Nagarjuna. *The Fundamental Wisdom of the Middle Way*. Trans. Jay L. Garfield. Oxford: Oxford University Press, 1995. A contemporary translation of the fundamental text in the Madhyamaka School of Indian Buddhist philosophy.

Olivelle, Patrick, trans. *Upanisads*. Oxford: Oxford University Press, 1996. A new and fluent translation of the classical Upanishads with an informative and thorough introduction.

Prebisch, Charles S., and Tanaka, Kenneth K., eds. *The Faces of Buddhism in America*. Berkeley: University of California Press, 1998. A collection of essays by specialists in different aspects of American Buddhism.

Rahula, Walpola. *What the Buddha Taught*. New York: Grove Press, 1972. A concise and accessible introduction to the Buddha's teaching by a respected Sri Lankan monk.

Robinson, Richard H., and Johnson, Willard L. *The Buddhist Religion: A Historical Introduction*. 4th edition. Belmont, CA: Wadsworth, 1997. The newly revised edition of one of the standard historical introductions to the history of Buddhism.

Shunryu, Suzuki. *Zen Mind, Beginner's Mind*. New York: Weatherhill, 1976. A modern Zen classic, this book has functioned as a lively and thoughtful introduction to Zen for a generation of Zen practitioners.

Stein, R. A. *Tibetan Civilization*. Stanford: Stanford University Press, 1972. A fascinating and accessible survey of Tibetan culture by an authoritative French scholar.

Strong, John S. *The Experience of Buddhism: Sources and Interpretations*. Belmont, CA: Wadsworth, 1995. A rich and varied compendium of Buddhist sources, ranging all the way from classical India to contemporary America. Each selection is introduced by a brief commentary that situates the selection in the development of Buddhist history.

Suzuki, Daisetz T. *Zen and Japanese Culture*. Princeton: Princeton University Press, 1959. The most inclusive study of Zen by one of its most famous and influential interpreters in the West.

Tanahashi, Kazuo, ed. *Moon in a Dewdrop: Writings of Zen Master Dogen*. New York: North Point Press, 1985. Clear and eloquent translations of Dogen's major writings.

ten Grotenhuis, Elizabeth. *Japanese Mandalas: Representations of Sacred Geography*. Honolulu: University of Hawaii Press, 1999. An attractive and authoritative study of the use of mandalas in the Japanese tradition.

Watson, Burton, trans. *Cold Mountain: 100 Poems by the T'ang Poet Han-shan*. New York: Columbia University Press, 1970.

———, trans. *The Lotus Sutra*. New York: Columbia University Press, 1993. A translation of the Chinese version of one of the Mahayana's most influential sutras.

White, David Gordon, ed. *Tantra in Practice*. Princeton: Princeton University Press, 2000. An encyclopedic collection of texts and commentary related to the Tantric tradition in Asia.

Wright, Arthur F. *Buddhism in Chinese History*. Stanford: Stanford University Press, 1959. An authoritative and concise survey of the history of Chinese Buddhism.

Internet Resources

www.shambhala.com, www.wisdompubs.org, www.tricycle.com—these are web sites associated with Buddhist publishers.

www.sfzc.com—San Francisco Zen Center.

www.mro.org—Zen Mountain Monastery.

www.dharmanet.org/infoweb.html—a directory of Dharma centers.

www.tibetart.org—a useful site on Tibetan art.